Nurturing for Community
1995

306.85 Krueger, Caryl Waller
K

Single with children

Single with Children

Caryl Waller Krueger

Abingdon Press
Nashville

Single with Children

Copyright © 1993 by Caryl Waller Krueger

This book is printed on recycled, acid-free paper.

Library of Congress Cataloging-in-Publication Data

Krueger, Caryl Waller, 1929–
   Single with children / Caryl Waller Krueger.
     p. cm.
   Includes index.
   ISBN 0-687-38555-5 (alk. paper)
   1. Single parents—United States. 2. Children of single parents—United States. I. Title.
HQ759.915.K78 1993
306.85'6'0973—dc20
                                     93-18280
                                          CIP

93 94 95 96 97 98 99 00 01 — 10 9 8 7 6 5 4 3 2 1

The names, places, and some details in the stories in this book have been changed to protect these special families.

MANUFACTURED IN THE UNITED STATES OF AMERICA

To those courageous moms, dads, and children who have found happiness and fulfillment through being part of a loving single-parent family:

Amy, Andy, Anne, Carrie, Cassie, Cheri, Claire, Claudia, Connie, Corey, Curt, Debbie, Delores, Diane, Francesca, Gil, Ginger, Helen, Janet, Janice, Jim, Judy, Karen, Kathy, Linda, Lori, Marie, Mark, Michael, Nancy, Natasha, Patrick, Paul, Peggy, Rob, Roberta, Ruth, Sandy, Stacey, Tina, Trevor, Victoria,

and many others who chose to remain anonymous but spoke from the depth of their hearts.

CONTENTS

Maybe you didn't plan it this way, but . . .

THE PLAN WAS FOR A LOVELY WEDDING, THEN THE HONEYMOON condo, a successful career, the first house, darling children, and living happily ever after. Right? But somehow, it didn't turn out that way.

So, what is there to do about it? Many tears have been shed over such plans that went awry. Perhaps the right person just didn't come along, or perhaps the happy marriage was followed by a devastating divorce, or perhaps death destroyed the pretty picture.

Now, bitterness, grumbling, anger, frustration, and bewilderment take over your hectic days and lonely nights. Self-pity, guilt, and hatred become your everyday companions. Limited income thwarts your plans. You ask, "Is this what my life is going to be like?"

It might be, but it truly *does not have to be*. Many single parents are accepting their single status, conquering the frustrations, enjoying their children, and going ahead with their lives. Certainly they still experience challenges, successes and failures, good days and bad. Yet through their own resourcefulness, intelligence, and strength of character, they have good lives now and high hopes for the future. This book lets these successful single parents talk to you in their own words. Reading about their problems might help you put yours in perspective. Listen. Learn how you can be "single with children" and at the same time live a wonderful life.

Join me in getting to know some very special single parents.

Caryl Waller Krueger

CHAPTER ONE

Heart to Heart

The challenge of single parenting

DO YOU BELIEVE EVERYTHING you read? I hope not! With so many families nowadays headed by a single parent, the statistics are pouring out like Niagara Falls! And the statistics are filled with warnings about the bad effects of single parenting. If you read this cascade of so-called facts, you might be tempted to believe that everything ends in despair—and that assumption could easily drown you in depression. But there's a life-preserver being thrown to you!

Today there is new hope for single-parent families—new hope from single parents themselves who are defying the statistics. Certainly some of these bad-news statistics are valid, but some are downright wrong, and many are statistics that *you* and other parents are rapidly changing. So you don't have to be swept away by generalizations or discouraging prognoses.

Why can I say there is hope for single parents? Because in the past year I've learned about the lives of many one-parent families. I've visited them in their homes and workplaces, talked on the phone with them for hours, and interviewed them in person or by mail. Hundreds have taken the time to fill out my questionnaires and write me personal letters filled with stories about how they have solved problems. They've shared with me their challenges and solutions, and from this information I've found some keys to success, keys that are available to you in this book.

NOTHING'S BROKEN

A "broken" family? That term certainly sounds bad, but statistics show that a healthy one-parent family is far superior to an unhealthy two-parent family. A positive environment results in well-adjusted kids. Husband/wife relationships can become broken, but today's single parents are proving that the family doesn't need to be broken as well. Happy and intelligent youngsters *can* be the product of a home with just one adult.

Labels can harm. Sometimes when a teacher hears that a child is from a "broken home," warning lights go on, and the teacher visualizes the child as a possible troublemaker or one with deep-seated psychological problems. This is the start of a perfect scenario for a self-fulfilling prophecy.

Disadvantaged is another label society is quick to slap on a single-parent family. The dictionary definition of *family* has been expanded to include "a group with common interests." Certainly most single-parent families have the common interests of surviving and succeeding in life! The "disadvantaged" tag comes because a single-parent family often has economic problems plus flimsy relationships with the absent parent. But remember, broken homes with disadvantaged children no longer have to be the norm.

STATISTICS WORTH KNOWING

The last decade has seen an explosion of single parents. With over fourteen million children under age eighteen living with one parent, a single mom or dad is no longer an oddity. As one kindergartner asked a newcomer to his class, "Which do you like better: living with your mother or your daddy?" By the year 2000, it is predicted that more than half of all family units will be headed by only one parent!

Now, no one is saying that this is the *best situation* or the *easiest way* to raise kids. But it's what we're dealing with, so we might as well recognize the crisis and take action. That's the best way to help both the parents and the children.

Be aware of these factors:

☞ About one million youngsters are involved in a parental divorce each year.

☞ One-fourth of all children live with one parent or one grandparent, while the other three-fourths live with two natural parents, or a parent and a step-parent.

☞ In over 90 percent of single-parent families, the child lives with the mother.

☞ The majority of single mothers do not have funds for more than basic necessities. The median yearly income for a single mother varies, but it is dismally low. For white women, it is about $14,000; but for African American and Hispanic women, only about $8,000. This is a vital figure since only 15 percent of white children live with a single mother while 48 percent of African American children live with a single mother.

☞ Remarriage becomes less of a statistical possibility as women get older. As a woman reaches forty, there are 128 women for every 100 men.

☞ Half of all children eligible for child support don't get it—their child support plan is either nonexistent, insufficient, or an empty promise. On the other hand, a child living with a single father has more "extras" and a higher standard of living. This is because most men still earn higher wages than women.

These are some of the "givens" that this book addresses.

STATISTICS WORTH FORGETTING

The fact that you are reading a book about single parenting indicates a desire to do a good job with your family. Your child or children will not be part of the discouraging statistics because you're going to do more of the right things.

That's why I call these next statistics "worth forgetting."

Yes, research shows that children of single parents have more problems. These problems sometimes stem from living with insufficient income, belonging to a racial or ethnic minority group, or living with a parent who doesn't care, or one who cares but doesn't know how to parent.

When the National Association of Elementary School Principals studied 18,000 students from one-parent families, they found that these children achieved less and got into more trouble than children from two-parent homes. It also was interesting to note that youngsters from low-income two-parent homes outperformed youngsters from high-income single-parent homes.

A recent study by the *Journal of Research in Crime and Delinquency* showed that the proportion of single-parent families in an area predicts its rate of violent crimes. Money can mend some ills, but it's no replacement for caring parents.

This is what the National Commission on Children has said: "Rising rates of divorce, out-of-wedlock childbearing and absent parents are not just manifestations of alternative lifestyles, they are patterns of adult behavior that increase children's risk of negative consequences." So the question is how to reduce those risks.

The problems of children from one-parent families are ones that you should be aware of. *And awareness puts you in a position to fight against the statistics.* Statistics show that these children, in comparison with children from two-parent families:

☞ Stay in school a fewer number of years
☞ Get into more trouble with the law because of less supervision
☞ Have more problems with relationships and are more apt to have a divorce themselves in later years
☞ Suffer from poorer health or have mental problems
☞ Have more psychological and behavioral problems that could lead to their becoming single parents themselves

☞ Feel that marriage isn't important. (Today's no-fault divorces make it easier to dissolve a marriage than to dissolve a business partnership.)

☞ Suffer from lack of good role models

☞ Are more easily discouraged and achieve fewer of the goals they set for themselves

☞ Pick up alcohol, tobacco, and drug habits more easily

☞ Have less satisfying careers and have lower incomes

ATTENTION!

These don't have to be *your* children. You can meet and master these challenges. And this book will help you get started.

Although the chapter titles may not describe your situation, read through every chapter and get to know parents who are succeeding. You'll find comfort in their stories and the ways in which these parents find answers to their problems. You're sure to find both hope and productive solutions that will result in a better life for yourself and your family.

PARENTS SURVEYED TELL ALL!

The parents in my survey were quite varied as to their education, income, race, profession, number and age of children, and reason for being single. They openly shared their challenges and some of their solutions.

The majority of parents answering the survey were women. However, the most vocal parents were usually the men who complained that they were very much left out of the lives of their children.

Most women felt they were coping adequately. And an amazing 35 percent enjoyed single life more than their past married life, although they'd marry again if they found the "right person." The two biggest worries about remarriage were how to discipline children and how to manage family finances.

Time to accomplish things was a big constraint—but that's true even with two parents. Finding time to be with the children, finding time to be in a singles group, finding time to read, learning to juggle commitments—many parents knew what was important, but somehow couldn't get it all together in the time available.

Almost one-third talked about wanting to get more education and how difficult this is. So often, "lack of education" was to blame for low income. And nearly half felt the pressures of parenting to the point of overload.

It is interesting to see the way parents perceive their own personal problems. Each may see the same situation quite differently. My survey included several pairs of husbands and wives who are now divorced. You might think that the answers on their questionnaires would be similar. But no, even on paper some spouses can't agree!

One husband couldn't come up with any reason for the divorce. The wife stated unequivocally that it was due to his adultery, alcoholism, and abuse.

Each half of another pair stated that they hoped they'd remarry the other since they still loved their "ex" but didn't think the "ex" loved them. I'm hoping they'll communicate with each other!

It was common to find that a custodial mother stated that the father never took advantage of visitation, yet the father said the mother plotted to keep him from the children.

While the truth may be somewhere between these opposing views, these people were still hurting.

Five specific problems—described like hostile enemies— recurred throughout most every interview. These are the adversaries of many single parents: anger, frustration, loneliness, guilt, and lack of funds. Many parents are meeting these challenges by utilizing positive, practical techniques. So, let's take a closer look at these five enemies. (You'll find more help in chapter 9: "Survival!")

ANGER

Single parents feel anger in several directions: against a divorced mate or even against one who has died, against themselves for their situation, against their children who rely heavily on them. The anger takes form in apathy and emotional outbursts.

The loss of power and the accompanying feeling of helplessness can make a parent lash out in anger over the smallest things. Perhaps a mother feels that she understood and could manage life *before* the divorce or death; but now all the rules have been changed and everyone and everything is against her.

The anger over being solely responsible sometimes makes a parent place great responsibilities on a child too soon. Avoid calling a child "the man of the house" or "our little mother." This may serve the parent's needs, but it definitely is not what the child needs. It makes the child angry with the missing parent and the one on hand too.

But once the parent's anger is analyzed and understood, it can be controlled and eventually overcome. It is wise to channel or compartmentalize the anger—finding the reason for it and not letting it spill over into other areas. In some cases a parent finds new strength from this anger and a determination to do a good job. This "I'll show them" attitude is sometimes effective, but it is damaging if the parent's motive is to show up the other parent.

Certain types of anger end when the marriage ends. The custodial parent no longer has conflict with or interference from the absent parent, and thus she or he becomes more authoritative and consistent. In turn, the noncustodial parent feels the pressure is off, and he or she can be less authoritative and consistent, sometimes spoiling a visiting child. This in turn can bring on new anger from the custodial parent when the child returns home from the visit. What an unnecessary, vicious circle!

A parent needs to recognize that some things may not change, so being angry about them is merely time-consuming and emotionally draining. The angry parent needs to see what the anger is doing to herself or himself and to the child. Recognizing the destructive nature of anger will help a parent defuse it and dispose of it.

FRUSTRATION

Single parents should remember that people in two-parent families feel frustrated, too. The difference is that a married couple can talk about it with each other. So the single parent needs a surrogate ear (a relative, counselor, or friend) who will help ease the tension by merely listening—and perhaps not even suggesting solutions. We often already know the solution to our anxieties, but we just want to let someone else know how we feel.

Frustration goes hand in hand with depression. It is a heavy load to be a single/custodial parent, and often the parent's frustration is so evident that it depresses the children too. When a parent feels powerless and depressed, most of the systems that make a family work grind to a screeching halt. Considering and solving problems one at a time will get the family moving forward again.

Parents should be alert to depression in their children. The level of depression in youngsters is much higher in single-parent families. Thus the single parent must spend adequate time nurturing and giving emotional support. Show the child that you are aware of sadness or hurt. Ask if the child knows why he or she feels that way and then try to find appropriate solutions that build self-worth. Beware of ordering a child to "snap out of it." Just as *you* must work your way out of depression, so must the child.

The antidote for frustration and depression is achievement—and even the smallest success will do. If a single mother is frustrated by loss of power, she needs to learn to take care of herself and regain power. Just repairing a frayed lamp cord or learning how to pay the bills can help.

The father is often deemed to be the ogre in a divorce. The assumption is that he has strayed, or he hasn't helped with the parenting. Thus he is frustrated by loss of acceptance and being cut off from society. For his own well-being he needs to nurture new relationships with others at work and in leisure activities.

Whether it is a depressed and frustrated child or parent, knowing that someone else cares and will take the time to listen and advise is extremely important. It is essential to recognize something—even a small thing—that is going right and hang on to that knowledge. From that point, success can build on success.

LONELINESS

Children can be companionable and so can business associates, but beyond these, parents need social opportunities. In my survey only 4 percent of single parents belonged to a support group, and only 9 percent had a regular weekly activity with peers. That's unfortunate—and harmful!

A parent may feel that being away from a child for a social event is detrimental. But what is good for the well-being of the parent is good for the child. It is amazing what a supper out or a game of tennis can do for a parent's sagging spirit.

Loneliness isn't necessarily cured by a ring on the finger! But many singles, having been badly hurt once, shy away from reaching out again. This is a shame. But it's also unfortunate when a single parent, out of loneliness, quickly jumps into a new relationship.

Certainly it's nice to have someone to share the work of parenting, but mutual tastes and aspirations as well as all-important love should be the foremost reasons for marriage. But first one must love and respect oneself. Adding one lonely person to another lonely person may have some immediate benefits—but when the loneliness is gone, what do they have in common?

Sometimes grandparents are drawn into the family to ease the loneliness. This is acceptable for a short while, but combining the two families is not wise unless financial necessity leaves no other choice. If grandparents must become regular daily caregivers, they often abdicate their most important function which is enriching a child's life as an impartial confidante.

Loneliness that lingers for months or years can result in the greatest problem that children living with a single parent have: they are forced to grow up too soon. They are given adult tasks and responsibilities. In the case of a single mother, a son takes on some work of the father, and a daughter becomes the mother's "sister" or "best friend." This can upset family relationships by confusing the essential roles of parent and child as well as their mutual responsibilities.

It may sound trite, but the best advice for the lonely person is to keep busy. There are the children who need affection and attention, the home that can be improved for better living, the church or social service agency that needs volunteer help. A busy person has little time to wallow in self-pity! He or she soon finds that others have greater problems than loneliness.

GUILT

Sometimes we feel better if we can lay the blame on someone else or something else—or even ourselves. "I'm a single parent because my husband was no good." "I should have tried harder to keep the family together." "My job was the cause." We go over such lines and then indulge ourselves in the "What ifs." "What if I hadn't had a baby so soon?" "What if I hadn't had an affair?" "What if I'd worked harder and earned more?"

The "what ifs" are a form of mental recreation, but they rarely do any good at erasing guilt. A good response to guilt is to accept what has happened, to see what can be learned from the experience, and then to move on with life. Mulling over the past can result in inaction and thus more guilt.

A parent sometimes inadvertently makes a child feel guilty. This happens when the parent is not forthcoming about why the marriage ended. Children readily think they are the cause of the disaster. Even when a spouse dies, the children can feel they're to blame—perhaps at one time they were so upset they wished the parent dead. This guilt needs to be explained away each time it crops up.

Some children also feel guilty because they see themselves as a burden to the single parent. Remarks such as "You are the most important person in my life"; "I don't know what I'd do without you"; and "We're going to get through this together" can certainly reinforce a parent's loving need for the child. Don't let this kind of guilt go unchallenged.

Lack of Funds

Most women in my survey complained about how little money they had to spend on the family. In many cases, increased income would salve their wounds. But having more money can camouflage the real problems, such as learning to live independently or to creatively manage what money there is.

Women who have lived on their own before marriage and parenthood are much more confident of their money management skills as a single parent. Though their incomes are reduced because of the absence of a mate, they budget wisely and often don't feel strapped. Women who are divorced or widowed later in life have the biggest struggle.

According to my survey, 92 percent of single-custodial mothers say they have barely enough money for necessities, far too little for "extras," and absolutely none for a now-and-then luxury or unexpected expense. Their lives and checking accounts have taken a sudden turn downward. (The few mothers who had adequate funds were those who had purposely embarked on single parenthood through adoption.) Some help for these financially strapped women is coming from the workplace, but at a snail's pace. Work assignments that can be done at home mean less day care cost. Sometimes shared-time and part-time jobs are a help. And on-site day care keeps parent and child more in touch, making working time more productive and less stressful.

A disgraceful problem, though, is the lack of teeth in the child-support laws. Quicker and more fair settlements must be made, wages must be garnisheed, and failure to pay must be fought immediately. Also, if women had better quality day care and support groups, they would be able to devote more energy to their jobs, be more successful, and thus earn more.

Some states, such as Wisconsin, are combating child poverty by encouraging marriage. "Wedfare" provides higher benefits for low-income couples who marry or remain married (since marriage means fewer welfare cases). It will be interesting to follow the success of this program, which at this time is showing that "wedfare" costs are far lower than "welfare" costs.

In the past decade, being a single parent has lost much of its stigma. Of no comfort to the single parent is the fact that public opinion is now swinging back toward the side of the two-parent family. This is not so much for moral reasons but for the simple economics of high welfare costs and higher law enforcement expenditures. A single parent who is trying to succeed deserves appreciation, not criticism.

CHART YOUR PROGRESS

The parents whose stories appear in this book have fought these five enemies and won. Often the fight was bitter—a fight not won in a day—but the victory was always sweet.

So that you can keep track of your progress, I have prepared an easy-to-use chart for you. On a scale of 1-10, with 1 being totally overcome by the problem and 10 being successful in dealing with the problem, rate yourself today and then monthly for the next six months. If you read this book and take action in applying the ideas, I'm sure you'll see the numbers rise. Pay special attention to the "Keys for Success" at the end of each chapter.

	TODAY	END OF MO. 1	END OF MO. 2	END OF MO. 3	END OF MO. 4	END OF MO. 5	END OF MO. 6
Anger							
Frustration							
Loneliness							
Guilt							
Lack of funds							

A KEY FOR SUCCESS

There is no magic formula to being a good parent. It takes dedication and work. When the parent is strong, consistent, and positive in approach, the children adjust more easily to living in a single-parent household. What your child really wants is an honest and loving parent. And that can be you.

CHAPTER TWO

"I Was Divorced and Devastated"

The success story of a mother and daughter who are getting it all together

PEOPLE FROM ROCK-SOLID New England just don't get divorced. At least that's what Lauren Ainsley from Portland, Maine, had been told. People from New England are stubborn, proud, well-educated and they honor the flag, blueberry pie, marriage, and motherhood.

Lauren sat in her small office and peered at me over her half-glasses as she explained this to me. She laughed and said, "So, how come I'm divorced and now living in New Mexico with my daughter Kate? I guess I trusted that everyone else honored the flag, blueberry pie, marriage, and motherhood as much as I did. Was I ever fooled!"

She leaned back in her chair, rearranged the reports on her desk, and turned a framed photo of a winsome, freckled face toward me. "That's Kate, and I want her to meet you; but for now, let me tell you why I left safe, stodgy New England to work at a chemistry lab in the Wild West.

"Let's not blame anything on my parents. They're super. They raised me and my two younger brothers to enjoy the outdoors, to trust and love one another, to believe in the goodness of people, and to value learning and hard work. I went off to college pursuing a degree in chemistry, but I quickly realized that a lot of students were more interested in pursuing marriage. Everyone was pairing off, but not finding 'Mr. Right' didn't bother me. I was sure he was out there somewhere, and I knew I'd find him sooner or later.

"So following graduation I got a job in my field and felt pretty content with my life. I lived on my own; I bought a car; I found a condo I liked. But, after a couple of years, life seemed to be at a standstill for me. I wasn't into the singles scene, but when a friend from work suggested we go to this neat place for a drink before going home, I agreed. I hardly thought I'd meet the man of my dreams in a bar, but I did. I couldn't believe how great he was, nor could I believe his occupation—he owned the gun shop next door to the bar. This was not the kind of man mother expected me to bring home for Sunday dinner!

"Still, Mack was so attractive and funny. And when I did let him meet my folks, they were totally charmed. Although I had always told myself I wouldn't live with a guy before marriage, he soon was living with me in the condo. I don't even remember how we agreed on that. Here I was, a logical, conservative, science-oriented person—hopelessly in love with someone I hardly knew.

"Mack had many friends. He also had an ex-wife and two sons. He described her as 'the unreasonable one,' but he did love his sons and that was a good sign to me. So when his divorce was final, we married. We had happy times together, and I really thought this was going to work.

"Oh yes, I was closing my eyes to his faults. He would

exclude me from many of his social activities. I didn't mind him taking a weekly night out with the guys, but I didn't like a night out with the guys *and* gals. And when he'd come home at all hours of the night, he resented my asking what he'd been doing.

"When I became pregnant, our relationship suddenly grew closer. I was thrilled, and he seemed to be too. He enjoyed his young sons when they visited us, and he hoped we'd have a girl. Those first months were the greatest. Then, near the end of the pregnancy, he became remote again.

"Kate was born, and I hoped he'd be at home more to help me during his free time; but his nightly wanderings became more frequent. My suspicions grew as he became increasingly deceptive about his companions and vague about his where-abouts. Finally, after months of trying to make home life more exciting, I could no longer stand his coming home at four in the morning. When I confronted him with my fears, he admitted his infidelity. I was so hurt and angry that I asked him to move out. He did, and he moved right in with a girlfriend named Shirley.

"The only good thing about this mess was that Kate was too young to know what was going on. She didn't understand the shouting, the accusations, the excuses. After he'd been out of the condo for a few months, Mack began phoning me now and then, saying he wanted to know about Kate. I learned later that he'd had an argument with Shirley, and she'd kicked him out. Since he had little income, he had no good place to go except the gun shop.

"Then, just a few weeks before Christmas he began calling almost every day. He admitted that his business—the gun shop—was in trouble. He said he missed me and Kate. She was over a year old by now and I so much wanted her to have a real daddy. Christmas is my favorite holiday, and I wasn't looking forward to Christmas alone with a toddler. My folks had retired to New Mexico since my brother and his wife lived there. They all really liked the climate and life-style. My other brother was also out-of-state, so I really had no one to enjoy the holidays with.

"So when Mack kept calling, I melted. He promised to be faithful and begged for another chance. Again I trusted what he said and let him move back in. That was some Christmas! Kate was just the right age to enjoy all the fun and gifts. And I was just trusting enough to think that Mack really meant what he said. I took a week of my vacation and we walked in the snow, took Kate sledding, went caroling with our neighbors, enjoyed my office party, and even had a romantic night out with friends.

"About the first week of January, when the tree came down and the parties ended, it was back to work for me, and back to his old tricks for Mack. He wasn't working, he wasn't sleeping at our place, but he was out playing. When he'd come home in the early morning, there was no hiding the fact that he'd been with another woman. I figured it was Shirley again.

"I felt so betrayed that I did something that still surprises me. One night Mack suddenly left immediately after dinner. Because I'd had enough of these games, I gathered up Kate, got in my car, and followed his old pick-up truck. Sure enough, he headed straight for Shirley's and pulled right up in front of her trailer home. I parked down the block and cried and cried. Then I got just plain mad. I didn't like being taken for a fool. So I decided to go and ring the doorbell.

"When I got to the door, it was open, so I walked right in with Kate clinging to my neck. It was like some cheap B-movie. A trail of clothing led to a back room. Kate babbled, 'Look,

Daddy shoe.' Mack heard us and walked out stark naked! I was surprised and Kate just clapped her hands.

"I boldly shouted, 'Get dressed and come home right now.' He wasn't a bit sheepish when he arrived at the condo a few minutes later. It was then that I knew I didn't really know this man. Quickly we gathered up all his possessions and away he went—probably back to Shirley.

"Then reality set in. I was devastated and wanted to run away—anywhere away from that New England town. But as the days came and went, I realized that I was now the sole support for my child and I had a job and a home right where I was. I'd done nothing wrong, so why should I run and hide?

"The biggest hurt was to my self-esteem. I'd been used to successes in my personal and business life. Now my feeling of self-worth was definitely in the toilet. I had to figure out the direction of my life totally on my own. Again I thought of running off to my parents, but I realized that would only postpone my recovery.

"I soon found that Mack had indeed moved in with Shirley. One day he called, begging me for a favor. I didn't want to talk with him, but I listened. For his weekend visitations with his sons, his first wife Jill wouldn't let the boys stay overnight at Shirley's. So it was worked out that Mack would have the boys all day Saturday, then drop them at my place on Saturday nights and Jill would pick them up Sunday morning.

"It was a weird arrangement, but it worked. In that way I still got to see the boys, and Kate would see Mack for a little while. That seemed to satisfy her toddler desire for 'Daddy.' It also meant that I got to know Jill—'the unreasonable woman' by Mack's description. She turned out to be quite reasonable, quite pleasant, and eventually a friend. We had many things in common, including a charming man who was a rotten husband.

"Our divorce didn't move along with the speed of light, but by now I'd regained my senses and some feeling of stability. With good legal help, the divorce was written to contain provisions that were good for me and for Kate. But even while the divorce was becoming final, I had to learn to like myself again. I mean, I doubted my judgment-making ability, and I felt unwanted. So, I set about to find peace with myself and just as important, peace with Mack."

On another day when we talked at her home, Lauren shared how that change came about. Kate, now seven, was off swimming with friends. The house had an orderly, contemporary look, yet it was obvious that a little girl was in residence. Her school work covered a bulletin board in the family room. On a shelf nearby, two fish and a cat seemed to be living in harmony, awaiting Kate's return. Her room was filled with books, ballet posters, and educational toys. And the living room had reading chairs for mother and daughter. In the garage was a rack that held two shiny bikes, and the view out the window showed a backyard with the usual play equipment plus some vegetables struggling in the southwest heat. It all came together to present a cozy feeling of home, not just a place of refuge from life with Mack.

As we settled in chairs and sipped cold lemonade, Lauren told me about her next steps. "During our marriage, Mack and I had tried counseling, but since he would never admit to any problems, it didn't accomplish much. But I knew I needed it for myself after the divorce. It certainly helped me sort out things in the years that I remained living in the same town with him. At the start I felt like the most worthless person in the world. I asked, 'If I was lovable, if I was good to him, if I was a good mother, why did he leave me?' I tried to figure out what was wrong with *me*—until I finally realized that the problem wasn't mine, but his. He didn't know how to commit to anyone; his life was based on his selfish desires; he focused on what pleased him and made him feel good, without concern for anyone else.

"It takes me three seconds to say that, but it took me three long years to understand it. Finally, I didn't hate him anymore, I just felt sorry for him with all his problems. I wasn't totally out of the woods, but I now felt I could move ahead on my own.

"I'd been offered a job out here two years after the divorce; but I was still confused and hurt, and I turned it down. Then two years ago, an even better job became available. This time I was ready to grab it. My condo sold quickly, and Mack even came by to help us pack up and to say good-bye to Kate. She and I drove across the country to a new job, a new house of our very own, and a new and wonderful way of life.

"Here I have the support of family and a wonderful group of friends—even though at this point I find myself *giving* more support than receiving it. My job pays me adequately, and Mack sends a child support check every month. I'll say that for him, he only missed a payment one time. And he'd usually call when the check was going to be late. It turned out he never owned the gun shop, so he got out of that and into construction, and he seems to be happier doing that.

"Yes, Mack finally married Shirley. Jill also remarried, but she still keeps in touch with me and is doing a good job with the two boys. Somehow we are all civil and almost friendly. Each summer Mack comes for a visit and tries to strengthen his relationship with Kate. She's a little shy at first, but it is a start of something positive.

"She's much more excited about the visit of her two half-brothers this coming summer. She always enjoyed their 'big-brothering' and now that she's older, we've planned a busy two weeks together. So, that's the story of one man, three wives, two sons, and one daughter."

Challenges

Lauren still has some problems to face, but she has regained her self-esteem and is on her way. The challenges she still deals with are:

1. Learning to trust others
2. Laying aside the anger
3. Carrying a burden alone
4. Building a career
5. Seeing that Kate has the advantages of a full life

For most divorced women, finances are the biggest challenge. Not so for Lauren, but she is certainly aware of limitations. You will read more about the financial problems of single mothers in chapter 6—the story of a mother who got off welfare through good planning and hard work.

Lauren gives much thought to the challenges that are foremost in her life. Because of her scientific background, she has an analytical approach to the problems. She really relishes each success along the way toward a solution.

Some Solutions

1. *Learning to trust others.*

When one has been deeply hurt and deceived, having faith in others isn't something that happens overnight. For twenty-some years Lauren had believed in people and the integrity of what they said. She thought she could easily identify a false person. Yet Mack's charm overwhelmed her, and she didn't see the problems beneath the surface.

Early in the marriage, she was willing to forgive his indiscretions and give him another chance—time and time again. Although suspicious, she preferred to put off a confrontation. Then, finding that she had misplaced her trust made her doubt her entire value system. Did she know how to tell right from wrong and good from evil? If she was wrong in something as big as marriage, could she ever be sure she was right about anything? Could she trust a friend? A business associate? A car-repair person? A new male acquaintance? Even her own daughter?

This learning to trust will be a gradual process—trust will at first be based only on hard facts or what she sees with her own eyes. Later it will be based on good faith. Each time her trust is well founded, her faith in humankind will increase.

It is fortunate for her that Kate is such an honest child right now. She is the one person her mother trusts totally. This places a large burden on a child who faces her teen years, knowing that she mustn't slip up. Perhaps by then Lauren's trust in herself will allow the youngster some youthful indiscretions without damaging their important bond.

I suggested to Lauren that she should actually write down those everyday decisions that depend on her trust. These could be a work decision based on someone else's research, the decision to let Kate spend a night at a friend's house, a decision on fabric for recovering an old chair. Then, later, she can go back over the list and see the great percentage of times her trust was well founded. This will increase her faith in her own decision-making processes.

---

2. *Laying aside the anger.*

This comes more easily to Lauren. She's still sometimes angry at herself as she recalls the bad choices she has made. However, her anger toward Mack is totally gone. She easily recognizes his problems—his womanizing, of course, and also his dishonesty and laziness.

The anger dissipated when she realized that Mack wasn't *her* problem. He was a grown man. While she could *see* the difficulties, she didn't have to solve them; they were his, not hers. She not only divorced *him*, she divorced his problems. She cares about what happens to him, but she is no longer responsible for him. She has responded to Mack in a positive way that shows her maturity.

For example, she is not responding as a vindictive ex-wife. Each year when he comes west to visit, she tells herself that Mack is Kate's father and that he deserves to see her and to know how she is growing up. She has been careful not to bad-mouth Mack, but just let the relationship grow from ground zero. Kate commented wisely for a seven-year-old: "I don't think he was a good husband or a good father, but I still want to see him. I'm a good daughter."

This year, Lauren is aware that Kate is more excited about a summer visit of her two half-brothers than she is about Mack's visit. First wife Jill trusts the boys in Lauren's care, but she won't permit them to be under-roof with Mack and third wife Shirley. For a week, Mack will also be on the scene—housed with Shirley at a motel a few miles away. It will be interesting to see how Mack interacts with the three young people. And Lauren will no doubt see Shirley for the first time since the divorce. That will be a test of self-control!

While there are many opportunities for anger in the visits ahead, Lauren zeroes in on what's important: she has a daughter who loves her, she has a good job, a nice home, friends and family who support her. So she's willing to share a little of this goodness with Mack.

3. *Carrying a burden alone.*

Here is a place where Lauren is gradually learning to shine. At first, it was hard work to be a single parent. She wasn't sure of herself or confident about her finances, and she was hesitant about her mothering skills.

She was wise enough to have good legal counsel at the time of her divorce. Many women are just so anxious to have the rotten marriage over that they don't recognize the opportunities for help. Some try the near-impossible: doing everything alone. Lauren recognized that if she was civil to Mack, if she let him have what he wanted (Shirley), then she could ask for things in return. Amazingly, first wife Jill had clued her in on some of these ideas. Who ever said ex-wives can't be friendly!

The child support Mack is able to pay is adequate to cover some basic needs. But beyond that, the divorce decree provides for financial extras that give Lauren peace of mind. Certain medical bills not covered by insurance, orthodontia, eye care, a stipulated amount for yearly travel for visits—these extras are to be paid by Mack. The one time that Mack missed a payment, Lauren's lawyer made immediate contact with sufficient pressure so that there's never been a missed payment since. Not having major money worries makes it easier for Lauren to cope on her own.

Beyond money, Lauren's job as a single parent has been made easier by her nearby family. She says, "I couldn't move near them until I knew I could be independent if need be. I didn't want my folks' pity or smothering love and I didn't want to revert to being their child again. So it was important to me that I was emotionally healed before I moved away from Maine. Now I enjoy the luxury of family and friends—this is the whipped cream on the cake for us."

These supportive people are very important to Lauren, and in turn, when there is a need among her circle, she is quick to do what she can. "It is great to receive loving care," she says, "but it's wonderful to be able to give it, too."

So many single parents think that they carry such a tremendous burden that they can't reach out to others. However, they are missing the satisfaction that comes from easing another's burdens. This outreach also helps in putting one's own problems in perspective. So much of what we do for one another doesn't involve spending money; it is the sharing of ideas, showing patience and understanding, being a good listener, doing small kind deeds. Lauren is able to both give and receive. The giving has increased her feeling of self-worth so that the receiving doesn't seem like a handout. "Raising a child alone isn't a burden, it's an opportunity to be loving and creative." This is easier to say when money is not an overwhelming problem, but even if it were, Lauren would find a way.

4. *Building a career.*

Lauren has the education that led her into a field full of opportunities. Now she's in the middle-income range. Still she has had to fight prejudice against women and single mothers. She is aware that each salary increase, small as it may be, is an important step for herself and those women who follow her in the chemistry field.

One problem she's had to face is her absence from work when Kate is not well. She is currently fighting for a plan at work that will combine the days allotted for family leave with the days for sick leave. This would mean that she would have a certain number of days each year she could be absent, and she would not have to specify if it were her health or her child's health that required the time off. This is important to her and to most other women in the company because they all want to be honest about the reason for absences.

Some of the men at the office look down on women who must stay home to care for a child, yet these men think nothing of their absences because of a stomachache or a mild cold. Lauren senses a subtle prejudice against women in the work place—as if women were not as seriously committed to their jobs as men. Since men sometimes are not involved in child care in their own families, they degrade these activities.

Even with occasional sick leave, she always gets her work done. In fact, when she's been absent or has a heavy workload, she comes in on Saturday morning with Kate. While Kate usually is content to play games alone, work in a coloring book, or write a short letter, she also likes to help by sharpening pencils for all the desks, running the copy machine for Lauren, and stapling reports. This togetherness helps Lauren stay on track at the office and also gives Kate the opportunity to see and understand what her mother does when they are apart.

Sometimes Lauren has to bring work home from the office; but now that Kate has some homework, they can sit down together at the dining room table, each doing her separate work. This is the beginning of establishing good study habits for Kate.

Lauren has been up-front in her discussions with her department head. She has made it clear that she's a loyal employee and that she wants increased responsibilities. At least four times yearly, she *asks* for a meeting to assess her progress. As the only wage earner in the family, she takes any suggestions very thoughtfully.

She's also made herself integral to her company by volunteering for some of the outreach projects—projects that the men seem hesitant to take on. Fund drives, Christmas toy collection, employee birthdays—these take some of her time, but they endear her to management. And she's smart enough to involve others in such projects so she can pass along the leadership to someone else after doing it for two or three years.

---

5. *Seeing that Kate has the advantages of a full life.*

This is foremost in Lauren's thinking now, but planning a definite future for Kate didn't seem important at first. However, the divorce lawyer was wise enough to cite the rising cost of a college education and to have the divorce decree provide that Mack pay half of these costs. A fund was established and, although it is growing, it now appears that it will not be adequate. So, Lauren is hoping for a raise early next year—and this would go directly into the fund.

For the present, the child support from Mack is very important. However, if something happened to Mack, Lauren has her own financial plan in place to provide for Kate's growing-up years. She says that it's very difficult to put aside this money and keep it "hands-off" when there is another more attractive or pressing need.

Lauren says that helping Kate grow up is so important that she makes definite plans for their time together. "We only have evenings and weekends for building good memories." They shop together, enjoy time at a pool, go for "walk talks," ride their bikes, play card and board games after supper, and do chores together. And every week there is some special excursion that takes a few hours of their time. They keep a list of things they want to do and places they want to go.

Her biggest concern for Kate's well-being and future happiness is that Kate is not able to observe a healthy husband/wife relationship. This problem is somewhat alleviated by time spent with grandparents and Lauren's married friends. But Lauren is correct in saying that this isn't the same as living with two parents on a day-to-day basis. For single-parent families, the question of role models is one that can't be emphasized too much.

KEYS TO SUCCESS

So many single parents hang on to the past, going over "what might have been." Lauren has realized that you can't go back, and you don't want to stand still, so you must go forward. With this realization, she doesn't waste time on self-pity or self-recrimination. She has a little phrase, "anger eats big," which means to her that you have to gracefully let the past go or it will eat up the present.

She was wise to stay in Maine until she had come to some decisions on her own: that Mack wasn't her concern anymore, that she was a capable woman, that she didn't have to run somewhere because of a bad marriage, that life didn't have to be an emotional roller coaster. Because she didn't run away but faced up to her personal crisis and settled it in a courageous manner, she solved many problems that made the move to New Mexico a logical and timely one.

She likes what a pediatrician told her some years ago. "Single parenting isn't more difficult, it's just different."

CHAPTER THREE

"He Died and Left Me Alone"

The survival story of a mom who lost two men in her life

A WARM NEBRASKA WIND blows through the open windows of the Nilson farmhouse. Nora is wearing a flowered dress and sits opposite me on a flowered couch, giving the impression of a bountiful garden in bloom.

You'd never know that this tidy house is headquarters for two active boys—Corey, age twelve, and Benjamin, age ten. During our conversation, Corey bursts in to ask if he can go down the road to play. Later, in contrast, Benjamin comes softly tiptoeing in, whispers in his mother's ear, and then tiptoes out again. Nora tells me he wants to know when I'll talk to him since he has some things to say. Yes, that will come in a little while. But first, Nora Nilson's story.

Nora and Jack met in high school and married the summer after graduation. The small farm was a wedding gift from Jack's parents, whose forebears had come to America from Norway many generations ago. It seemed natural to start a family right away. By Jack and Nora's sixth wedding anniversary, their sons were five and three years old, and Nora was pregnant again.

The boys, though small, would play outside each morning, helping feed the animals and watching their dad as he repaired farm machinery. Jack had a job in town in the afternoons and on weekends, which helped the family finances. Nora was taking night-school classes in nursing, a profession she chose because it would also be useful with her family—the most important consideration for her.

One day, she was in the house reading a textbook for that evening's class when she heard the boys screaming. As she reached the porch steps, she could guess what had happened. Jack had taken the old tractor out of the shed and misjudged the weight of the load he was pulling. As he made a too-sharp turn, the tractor began to tip, he fell off, and the tractor fell on top of him. As she raced to the tractor, the boys were no longer screaming. There was total silence as the three stood frozen, looking at the hand outstretched from under the machinery. By the time help arrived, Jack had died.

Now, seven years later, Nora still weeps as she tells this story. She runs her hand through her short-cropped hair, takes off her glasses, wipes her eyes, and then slowly adds, "And that's not all."

Regaining her composure, she recounts the series of tragedies that followed Jack's death. First, she had a miscarriage. Then her in-laws cut her out of their lives. They criticized her for having children too soon, causing Jack to work extra-hard—and thus they blamed her for his death. Next there was the crisis with Ben's heart. He had been born with a hole in his heart and had surgery as an infant. The year after Jack's death, further life-threatening surgery had to be performed.

Nora felt so alone, even though her sister came to help her through the ordeal.

She continued, "After Ben's recovery, family life became more normal. Two years ago I met someone I'd known in school, Howie, and we began dating. That caused some behavior problems with the boys, but in general, our foursome functioned to everyone's advantage. Then tragedy struck again. The relationship ended when Howie was diagnosed with terminal cancer and died in just a few months."

Nora looked at me and smiled through her tears, saying, "I've really been through it, haven't I!"

It has been a year now since Howie's death, and Nora volunteers that she has survived and is actually content with life. She takes me on a walk through the house. The kitchen refrigerator has the mandatory school papers and notices on it, plus photos of the boys playing baseball. In a sunny corner of the kitchen there's an oak table with flowered place mats and a Bible on it. The unneeded dining room has been converted into an activities room for all the family. There are books to read, games to play, a racing car set on the floor, and a TV in one corner. The three upstairs bedrooms are small, but bright posters cover the walls of the boys' rooms. Watercolors of flowers are in Nora's room. The hall walls are covered with framed photos, including many of Jack and the family.

How did Nora survive? She laughs and says, "I didn't have a choice. Jack and I loved having a family, and at the beginning I did what had to be done out of duty to him. Now I do it for myself and because it's the right thing to do."

This "right thing" is the establishment of a deeply caring sense of family. Nora realized right off that she couldn't be both mother and father, but that she *could* be a very good mother. "I keep going, knowing that my mothering will get easier; by the time the boys finish school, I'll have more time to myself. But right now, it's mainly family and work, work and family."

Work means her job. She never had the time or money to finish her nursing classes, but she did have enough training to work in the health and physical education department of a private school in the large town forty minutes away. So her hours somewhat conform to the boys' hours at the country school they attend.

But until Ben had fully recovered from his operation and was in kindergarten, she stayed at home caring for him and taking some classes by mail. This meant she used up the insurance money and their small savings.

I asked Nora about financial help from relatives. She shook her head and said, "My own parents have been supportive in many ways but are not able to help financially." She stared at her lap and added, "There continues to be little input from the in-laws. That relationship remains cold even though they live nearby. Somehow, the anger over their son's death was transferred to me and the boys."

But she insists that even without relatives to help, she isn't doing it all alone. "I have a very close relationship with God. I talk to him. I listen to him. With the boys I read the Bible each morning at breakfast, and we pray to God to help us through the day. I couldn't have done this without God's help. I wasn't much on praying before Jack died, but I've gotten real good at it in the years since."

Ben comes quietly into the room again. "Is it my turn to talk soon?" His appealing sun-tanned face and his desire to talk about his family prompts Nora to go into the kitchen "to check on dinner" so I can talk with Ben.

When we're alone he announces proudly, "I have a mended heart, I'm dyslexic, and I am the pitcher on the baseball team."

We talk about baseball first. He and the boys who live nearby have made a baseball field in an unused pasture down the road. It's their own "Field of Dreams."

He says in an engaging way that his mom wasn't much help on teaching him how to throw strikes, but that Howie was. "That was Mom's boyfriend, you know. He died, too." He admits to liking Howie and missing him, but says that he has more time with Mom now that Howie doesn't come around.

"She has to help me with my homework, and we have these boring reading exercises to do. I used to hate them and put up a big stink about doing them, but Howie said I'd be worth nothing if I didn't learn how to read well. So I do them."

It is clear that Ben benefited from Howie's being part of the family circle. Ben was so young when his father died that he barely remembers him. But he seems to remember the accident and he tells me about it in graphic detail.

Before I can respond, he says, "Daddy is in heaven. I'm gonna see him again a long time from now, and so I don't want him to be ashamed of me." It's clear that Nora has gone over the subject of death and life with him, and he is at present satisfied with the answers.

Corey returns, brushes off his jeans and sits carefully on the edge of the flowered sofa. Immediately he takes over the conversation in a big-brother manner, telling Ben to "go help Mom." Corey explains, "I have to look out for him, tell him what to do, help him grow up—you know."

And that is what Corey seems to do. He looks out for Ben, and he looks out for Nora. However, when I ask about his dad or Howie, he refuses to give more than a shrug of his shoulders. Then, looking down at his hands he says, "I don't know what's going on, but I hope someone does. I try to be good, so why does all this bad stuff happen to me?" Clearly he has some important unanswered questions about the tragedies in his life.

We talk about school, where he does above-average work. "I may have to support Ben and my mom someday," he says with shy pride. I reassure him that Ben will not be a burden to him and that his mother has plans for upgrading her credentials and increasing her earnings so that there will be some funds for college. He nods and says with a sigh, "That's good—if it happens."

When Nora and I have an opportunity to talk privately, we consider some of the problems she faces.

Challenges

1. Being a single mother with two very active boys
2. Facing up to death and grief
3. Encouraging further education
4. Handling loneliness for herself
5. Improving the boys' reaction to her dating

Some Solutions

1. *Being a single mother with two very active boys.*

Nora has found that she can actually take part in, and enjoy, much of the "man stuff" that Jack, and then Howie, did with the boys. But she's wise enough not to try to be two parents in one.

Through the physical education department at the school, she is learning so much about sports that Corey has asked if she'd like to be an assistant coach for his soccer team next year. She smiles and says, "That's a brave suggestion—for a boy to try to get his mom involved."

Nora is aware of Corey's feeling that he thinks he should be "the man in the family." This has been even more of a problem since Howie died. "When Howie was here for a meal, we'd always have him sit in Jack's place—at the head of the table. No one had sat there for five years. I noticed that Corey would act up a lot at these meals, and it didn't occur to me at first that he felt this was an affront to his dad. Now I see that we can alternate sitting there.

"Rather than my making all the decisions, we take turns being in charge of things like how to get chores done, where to go on an excursion, what needs to be bought first, how much homework help to give, how to correct our faults. This works well for the boys. Without making a special point of it, they are learning self-discipline and leadership. When something has to be decided, I sometimes ask what they think Jack or Howie would have suggested."

Nora is wise not to let either boy try to take the place of a missing husband. Each relationship is special. Certainly the boys need male role models, but fortunately their minister (a happily married father of two girls) includes Corey and Ben in his family's activities. In this way he has gotten to know them well, and they trust him and enjoy talking and being with him.

With Corey, Nora has had some conversations about premarital sex, AIDS, dating, and so forth. He has shrugged it off by saying that it is "too soon and he isn't interested in girls," but Nora noticed that he did read the booklets she gave him. She says that some of these discussions would be easier for a father to handle, but she's determined to keep the communication going.

A male school counselor has taken a special interest in Corey and has talked with him about his educational aims. Also, from time to time he's brought the conversation around to other, more personal matters. Nora is encouraging this since it will give Corey one more male confidante.

But the boys still need additional male role models. Living in a community of families would help provide this, but at present the Nilsons live forty minutes from her job, the high school the boys will eventually attend, the church which offers many family events, and most organized activities. Grandparents are even farther away. Nora needs to think about renting or selling the farm and moving into town. The boys could then take part in more activities and interact with other families and especially other adult men.

At this point in their lives, being part of an extended family and a caring community is extremely important.

2. *Facing up to death and grief.*

Nora makes sure that she keeps memories of the past alive and speaks positively about those who have died. "At least I don't have the problem of most divorced parents—trying not to bad-mouth each other," she says with some glee. "I've known two wonderful men who cared about me and the boys.

"My religion has given me wonderful encouragement. The church has really been a help in counseling the boys. I think Ben is through the worst of it, but Corey still needs more help so that he can talk easily about Jack and Howie.

"Our family photos on all the upstairs walls are one way of keeping memories alive. And we talk about what Jack wanted for the boys and his aims for this farm. We rent out the land right now, but Corey talks about making the farm run in a profitable way someday. He's the kid who could do that."

It's clear that Corey is confused by the loss of his father, and to a lesser extent, Howie. And Benjamin may have more questions about these tragedies as he grows older. Both boys need the reassurance that they did not cause their father's death even though they observed it.

One day, about two years after Jack's death, Ben asked his mother if she thought Jack was really dead or that maybe he had recovered but had lost his memory and thus couldn't find them. This is typical. Some children think that if they are very, very good the parent will return. Nora needs to help the boys know that Jack will not one day walk in the door and that there is nothing they can do to reverse the process and bring the missing parent back again.

Tied in with death is a child's concern about the future. The remaining parent must carefully reassure a child that his needs for loving care, food, and housing will continue to be supplied. Sometimes this is a difficult promise for a parent when funds are short, but a lessening of the child's concerns is important.

With the strain and sorrow of the miscarriage followed by Ben's illness and surgery, Nora and her family may not have had time to truly grieve for Jack and then recover. They just got stuck at the level of disbelief that follows a death. It's important that they face up to the changes in their lives without Jack or Howie. And it's important that they talk about their life as it is now without these men to help them through the hard times.

Certainly Nora's faith and the boys' religious training is a great support here—a good reason to be living nearer the church family.

3. *Encouraging further education.*

It was always Nora and Jack's hope that the boys could go to college. Nora sadly says, "Any college for the boys will be a financial stretch for me. The schools are too far from here for them to live at home. So I face room and board in addition to the tuition.

"When he becomes a teen, Corey thinks he can work in the summers to save up. He's the determined one. I can't tell about Ben yet. The dyslexia is something we're working on—his grades aren't the greatest. Still, he has such a sweet personality. I know I have to let him grow up and take his lumps, but I have the tendency to protect him after all he's been through. I know that not everyone needs college to have a successful life.

"I'm talking to the counselor where I work so that I can see other options for him. He's good with his hands like his dad, so maybe something mechanical would be good for him. I'm going to check on vocational schools. Right now, I am encouraging him to stand on his own and lean a little less on me for everything. His baseball games are part of this growing up."

At present Nora needs to be very diligent in following the special education suggestions concerning Ben's dyslexia. It isn't a matter of whether or not Ben enjoys the exercises. She needs to set aside about twenty minutes each day—perhaps before dinner when Ben isn't tired—and consistently follow the recommendations. This small investment could make a big difference in Ben's ultimate educational choices.

4. *Handling loneliness for herself.*

Although Nora demands very little for herself, she recognizes that for her own well-being, she needs to have some extras in her life. Her continued work toward a nursing degree is just one part of this. She will be in her late thirties when the boys go off on their own, and she says she plans to "really live" then.

She needs to "really live" now, too. To that end, she's friends with a group of women who have a "night out" once a month. Now that Corey and Ben can be left alone in the evening, she's also taking an active interest in her church, working on the fellowship committee and singing in the choir. She has just subscribed to two monthly magazines in order to broaden her interests.

Despite her problems, Nora considers herself blessed. She has a job, good health, and two very active sons. Of single parenting she says, "It's hard to be the one making most of the decisions—it's easier when two can talk it over." She also finds that when one of the boys is too sick to leave alone and she can't take off from work, there isn't a good way to care for the youngster. She often pays fifty dollars a day for someone to come and look after the child. "This can put a big hole in your budget."

With the boys' help she's planted a garden to cut down on food bills. She finds gardening a pleasant change of pace from her work. Watering and weeding give her time to plan and dream.

One thing she really misses is conversation with adults. She and Jack regularly drove together in their pick-up to the nearest town for his afternoon job, or her classes, or errands. She still misses those hours of talk. Because her work at the private school is mostly health and physical education record-keeping, plus dealing with sick youngsters as a nurse's aide, she'd like to eventually put together a network of people she could talk with on the phone when she wanted to hear an adult voice. She has a small circle of friends, but at present no best friend or confidante.

In this problem category, Nora is making real strides, but she needs to recognize that having a man around the house is not necessarily the answer to her feelings of loneliness. She went from her father's house to her husband's house, through hard times alone, and then into the relationship with Howie. When she met Howie, she was ready to make him the center of all her activities. Now she's working hard at being a whole person herself.

Again, a move into town would open many social doors. But she clings to the farm where she was a bride and life was beautiful. Those days are now gone and she needs to look forward, not backward.

5. *Improving the boys' reaction to her dating.*

Nora would enjoy male companionship—and, she says, eventual marriage. But for the present, she's decided not to date. She says *she* has gotten over the grief and anger of Howie's death, but she thinks the boys need some breathing time. She is not making the mistake that many lonely singles do: seeing marriage as the best way to fill the void.

Nora is intimidated by the boys on this point. They cling to her and want her for themselves.

She knows that any new relationships are certainly not replacements for Jack or Howie and all they meant to her and the boys. Regarding these deaths, the boys have joked that anyone their mom loves dies. This joke hides their own fears that they could die, too.

At present, she thinks she's dealt with her anger, but she's not sure she has "forgiven" these men for dying and leaving her alone. This must be the next step.

❖   ❖   ❖

"Some folks say I've had a hard time, but I know many single parents who are having a much harder time. At least I don't have the pain, frustrations, and anger of divorce pulling at me and the kids."

And then there are some folks (such as her in-laws) who are critical of her staying on at the farm or occasionally dating. She responds with a modification of the old saying. She says, "Don't criticize me until you walk in my shoes."

Keys to Success

There are many things we can all learn from Nora Nilson. She is succeeding as a single parent for many reasons. She knows that her children depend on her, so she fights loneliness and depression with the determination to do her best. And her strong faith has been an immeasurable asset.

She's aware of the problems—in fact she keeps a list of them—and she regularly works on solutions. She is giving her sons full lives despite the lack of a father, despite the health and learning problems, despite their out-of-the-way country home.

Looking ahead is another key to her success. Although the boys are still in grade school, she thinks and talks about the future.

Although she is aware of the statistics concerning children of single parents, she is determined to beat those statistics. Her sons are not going to be deprived of love, family structure, or goals, nor are they going to get into more trouble than two-parent kids. "The statistics are talking about what's average—kids with no direction and no respect—my family is going to be different."

One big change for the better that she could make is to move. A move would not necessarily preclude her desire to retain ownership of the farm to pass on to the boys, especially to Corey. But for her own life and future, it is something she should consider.

Determination, faith, problem-solving skills, and keeping an eye on the future have brought and will continue to bring success to this courageous woman.

CHAPTER FOUR

"They Didn't Think a Man Could Do It"

How a dad copes with day-to-day parenting

TROY SITS IN A ROCKER ON THE porch of the old house set on a tree-lined street in an Oregon college town. He's still in his twenties but as he rocks, he talks with a sageness far beyond his years.

"Tracy and I were the ideal couple. Everyone said we were meant to be husband and wife—our names sounded so good together. We met in high school, started going steady the night of the senior prom, and then talked our parents into letting us go to the same college. At first we lived in dorms miles apart. During our freshman year we got engaged and by our sophomore year we'd bought a car together so we could see each other more often. During our junior year we lived with four other students in a ramshackle house—actually it was this house, but it was in really bad condition. By our senior year, we started to plan the long-awaited wedding.

"The day after graduation was the big event—all our families, our brothers and sisters and cousins, plus our college friends witnessed our commitment to love each other for the rest of our lives. What a day, what a party—I still have hundreds of leftover paper napkins that say Tracy and Troy!"

Troy shuts his eyes in pain, cocks his head as if listening for something, then continues his story. "That first year was great. We'd both found jobs downtown, so we usually had lunch together in the park. At night we'd goof around with our friends, go bowling, go to movies, or just look at TV. We'd rented this same old house, but now it was just for the two of us. It had a couple of extra bedrooms upstairs, but we just closed the doors and pretended they weren't there.

"We weren't getting ahead financially, but that didn't matter . . . we were young and in love. When you're twenty-two and having fun, not much else matters. We had jobs, we were proud of ourselves, we had the world by the tail.

"Then it happened. Tracy became pregnant. Sure, we wanted kids for those extra rooms, but not just yet. We were in a daze at first. We'd been so careful. How did it happen? We talked about an abortion, but we each knew we couldn't do that. This was a baby, something we'd created ourselves. And remember, we were very proud of what we ourselves could do.

"We decided to make the best of it. Our parents reminded us that they'd been young when they first had children and that they'd managed to still have a great life together. I believed that and I think Tracy did too, at least at first. The folks talked a lot about our new responsibilities. We listened and tried to get ready for parenthood.

"So the fun continued. But now it was the fun of fixing up the old house, furnishing a baby room, setting aside some money for when Tracy couldn't work. She liked all the showers and baby clothes and toys, and we'd often sit on the floor of the nursery and look at all the baby stuff. But Tracy was sometimes sad—maybe melancholy—but I thought it was just the weight gain and the fear of labor.

"When the time came for the baby to be born and we were at the hospital, she wouldn't let go of my hand. Over and over she said, 'Troy, I love *you*.' She always accented the word *you*. I told her how much I loved her, and she began to cry. She cried all through the delivery, but the doc said that was normal for some women.

"We'd chosen the names Trina and Trevor, and this baby was Trevor. They came home in forty-eight hours and Tracy seemed to be happier now, setting up the routine of the day, opening the gifts that arrived, entertaining the visitors who came to see the baby. That was fine with me since I was doing some overtime work in order to help with the bills.

"Our first really big argument came about a month later. I asked Tracy when she thought she'd go back to work. She said, 'Never' and stormed out of the room. I followed her, shouting, 'What does that mean?' That woke the baby and started him screaming. We hardly spoke for three days.

"At the end of each week we had the custom of going over our finances. It was pretty grim, but I didn't mention her working. She said I'd spent too much money on an old house that wasn't even ours. By now, we had a lease with option to buy, and I was hoping we could start owning the house—but I knew we couldn't do it without two incomes.

"Although we'd talked before about earning enough to buy the house, Tracy sulked when the subject now came up. She said I was asking too much of her, so I just kept quiet for a couple months.

"Trevor was an easy baby, and suddenly Tracy said she was bored at home and wanted to look for a really interesting job, even though she could have gone back to her former job in personnel. This seemed like a good idea to me since she was restless at home and we really needed the extra cash.

"Almost every day she'd get a babysitter and go out job hunting, then lunch with a friend and go shopping. When I'd offer to help with Trevor, she said that men didn't really understand such things. It was as if she felt proud about doing something that I couldn't do: care for a baby for more than a few minutes.

"She was nursing the baby even though she hated doing it. But she pointed out that this was another thing I couldn't do. She talked about what a sacrifice it would be if she found the job she was looking for and the baby would have to go on formula. She explained to me all the ways the baby would suffer with two working parents. I was confused as to whether she really wanted to work or stay home. Certainly it would be hard for us to work all day and then come home and spend time with the baby; but I knew others had done it, and I assumed we could learn to do it too.

"The next month she began talking about our childless friends who were still having fun. So I made a real effort to spend time with her, and we had a 'date night' each week. When we came home from a fun evening out, she'd moan that nothing good would happen for another seven days. It was then I suggested some family counseling. That resulted in the next big blow-up and again, no conversation for several days. I felt she was punishing me for getting her pregnant.

"Then one night when I came home she was really excited. That afternoon she had been interviewed for a job at a small clothing design firm in a town about forty miles away. She would be in charge of personnel, selecting models, and maybe even doing some modeling herself. She'd hear back in two weeks—and during those two weeks she took off ten pounds, highlighted her hair color, and spent every waking moment with the baby, ignoring me when I tried to join in.

"It was a big day when she got the job. We went out and celebrated. She'd already arranged pretty good day care for Trevor, and soon it seemed we were back on track as a couple and as a family. In a few months we went ahead and bought this house, since we again had two incomes.

"Well, in three months she'd had a raise and was traveling to a big garment show in another state. Then the roof fell in—actually two roofs fell in at the same time.

"While she was away, we had a big wind storm. Part of the roof tore off. I was busy working, and caring for the baby at night. I couldn't do the repair myself so I had to hire someone— and that took money. When Tracy called the next day, she first told me about how exciting her work was. Then I told her what had happened.

"That's when the second roof fell in. She'd been asked by her company to stay on another few days—and did I mind? I told her I was getting the hang of it, even though Trevor was fussy with teething. And I told her how proud I was of her but that I missed her. All she said was, 'Oh, you'll get over that.'

"Those words didn't mean much to me at the time, but three days later she came home during the day while I was at work. When I arrived home, I found she'd packed all her personal belongings. She'd left a scribbled note with the sitter saying I could have all the wedding gifts—and the baby!

"Through her employer I tracked her down in another state. All she said was that she couldn't stand the pressure, marriage was no fun, motherhood was a strain, and that she was filing for a divorce when she had some free time. So that's how I became a single father."

He smiled and added, "I wasn't too good at fathering at first but after nearly three years, I'm as good as any mother. Let me show you." He leapt out of the rocker, went into the house, and soon returned with Trevor, just up from his nap. The toddler climbed into his father's lap, and they sat together quietly rocking and snuggling.

Later, Troy told me of the first years and the parenting problems he faced. The divorce didn't take place right away; but when it did, it went smoothly. But the child custody question wasn't finally determined so it still keeps popping up—it's a continuing battle. This is partly because Tracy's career has begun to bore her, and she thought it might be fun to be a mother of a bright little boy as opposed to a helpless infant. She dropped by several times over the course of the last year and took Trevor out for ice cream or a trip to the zoo. Troy noted that she never was content to just be with him at the house.

The judge was inclined to follow the tradition of giving children to the mother, but he finally gave Troy custody with liberal visiting rights for Tracy. Troy soon noticed that her visits became less and less frequent and were more like the visits of an aunt than a mother.

Troy was eager to cite his list of problems as a single father.

Challenges

1. The settlement of the custody question
2. Female role models for Trevor
3. Dating for companionship, not marriage
4. Obtaining good parenting information
5. Answering questions about "Mama"

Some Solutions

1. *The settlement of the custody question.*

Custody battles hurt everyone involved. Although he has custody now, Troy is concerned that Trevor could be taken from him; and thus he'd like it settled once-and-for-all. He has a good attorney for the times when Tracy decides to change her mind, but it's costly since she unexpectedly cancels the hearings. Since the divorce was not final for almost two years (during which Troy thought they'd reunite and Tracy was too busy with her job to talk about it), the custodial arrangement is a tenuous one.

The best interest of the child is what it's about. Troy wants sole custody; Tracy wants joint custody but not physical custody. In the back of Troy's mind is the worry that Tracy is impetuous and sometimes irrational in her reasoning. He doesn't want a situation where Trevor would be taken across the country by his mother and then not returned to him. He envisions the worst scenario of a parent kidnapping a child.

He says that Tracy is a good actress and can convince people that her work forced her to leave her child but now she is ready to assume some responsibility. Troy argues that he's come through the difficult infant years alone and deserves the right to have his son as he grows up. He says, "I don't want yo-yo parenting. I know that if she has Trevor, as soon as there's a problem, she'll give up as she did before."

Certainly Troy has demonstrated his ability to care for a child. He's eager to admit his prowess at reading stories, teaching toddler skills, selecting clothes, caring for Trevor when he's sick, getting stains out of the clothes, making nutritious meals, and being patient with all the questions of an active toddler.

Seeing Trevor "in action" certainly showed me that he isn't suffering from an inept or disinterested father. Troy says that since he doesn't have to spend time with a wife, he has lots of time to devote to his child. He admits that he wasn't too interested in the first months after Trevor was born but that he's more than made up for it in the last few years. This is how he puts it:

"Women—or at least women like Tracy—need to have areas of expertise. Just as I can program a computer or change a tire, Tracy could cook and care for the baby. We could have exchanged roles, but we were comfortable and I accepted this division of work.

"As much as she disliked infant care, she felt proud about doing things I couldn't do—getting pregnant, giving birth, nursing a baby. She lorded it over me and made this an area of mystery to me, holding it over me and even teasing me about it. It was as if we were competing for who could do the most for the baby. Having made that point very effectively, and closing me out of baby care, she then decided to show me how inadequate I was as a father. She just left me with the baby. But it turned out that I learned how to do it, and do it real well.

"Essentially she abandoned the two of us. She rarely called; she'd never tell me when she was dropping in—and when she did, she always found fault with the house or the food I had or the laundry or the way Trevor was dressed. Believe me, I was doing a good job, but she wouldn't admit it. Yet I felt that deep down I still loved her and wanted us to be a family, so I didn't rush the divorce. She was too busy to push for it either. So here we are now with a little boy who will soon be four years old. Aside from the first five months, he's spent all but a half dozen days with me, in my care or at day care. Why shouldn't he be totally mine?

"On the other hand, I'm willing for her to visit if she'd give me some advance notice, but I don't want her taking him away from this city. I just don't trust her."

Troy has just been asked by the court to submit a plan of implementation (how custody will work, visitation opportunities, travel, etc.), and this may bring a satisfying conclusion for both Troy and Tracy. By the time this book is published, the custody matter will be settled.

---

2. Female role models for Trevor.

Role models are important for all children. However, it is far easier for a man to find female role models than for a woman to find male ones. Trevor will be exposed to many women in day care, later in school, and in activities where it is common for women to serve as caregivers, teachers, and den mothers. Men are almost nonexistent in the elementary teaching field.

But Trevor will also need women on a less formal basis. A little girl living with a father would have the same need for closeness with a woman or women. He's tried to make friends with others on his street; but since it's an older neighborhood, many of the residents are senior citizens. It would be nice if one of these older women could become a "proxy" grandma for Trevor as he has no relatives nearby. That could benefit both families with companionship and opportunities for caring love.

Troy doesn't attend church, so he lacks that kind of support group. He's thinking of going to a "Parents Without Partners" meeting, and he may find some answers there. Among the group that he and Tracy used to socialize with, most are couples and few include him in the fun of the old carefree days.

Troy mentioned some of his skills as "woman stuff." When I asked him what he meant, he said, "Cooking and sewing and things that women know instinctively." I assured him that these were not instinctive and if he wanted, he could learn them through trial and error, through books and magazines, or through night school. Eventually he wants to teach Trevor these skills.

As we talked, I noted that it wasn't so much these skills but rather the traditional feminine qualities that he needed to be aware of in his dealing with Trevor. He had had little training in nurturing and no formal training in child care.

He reassured me that he is a good listener, he is generous with praise and kisses, and that he is teaching Trevor to be nurturing since a kitten adopted them a few months ago. This certainly indicates progress.

---

3. *Dating for companionship, not marriage.*

Dating often poses a problem for a single parent. Troy's predicament is that he's only interested in companionship at present. "Oh, if the absolutely right person came along, I'd marry again. But first I have to figure out what I did wrong the first time."

Troy shouldn't put all the blame on himself for the divorce. He and Tracy were immature when they married and had a baby. They hadn't gotten their goals for life beyond the "let's have fun" stage. And Tracy may have had some deep-seated anxieties about motherhood. This can't be undone now. Troy needs to go forward.

He says he only wants "a date now and then" because he's afraid of being hurt a second time. He's steeling himself against the pain by holding women at a safe distance. Eventually, he will want to be more open so that a relationship has an honest foundation on which to grow. For his sake—and Trevor's—he needs to be willing to love again.

Although Trevor occupies much of Troy's free time at present, there will come a time when Trevor requires less attention, and finally a time when he moves out of the old house in order to be on his own. What then for Troy?

He covers up his need for companionship by saying, "This old house would scare off any woman. I'm good at remodeling, and Trevor and I work at this most weekends. We're a team, we don't need a wimpish woman." The old house is proof of his abilities—the wood floors gleam, the walls are freshly painted, there is space for his work and space for Trevor's play—plus a fenced yard with a flower border. Perhaps there is somewhere a non-wimp female who will bring back the fun of married life and family life to these two males.

4. *Obtaining good parenting information.*

At first it amazed Troy that people didn't take him seriously when he had a parenting question. Certainly he had books to instruct him, and he had a pediatrician, but sometimes he had a "meat and potatoes" kind of question—the kind that women would discuss while sitting in the park watching the kids play. He was seriously interested in the "small talk" of being a parent.

He tells a funny—and sad—story about a morning in the park. "I had this day off since I'd worked overtime. So with eighteen-month-old Trevor in the stroller, we set off for a day outdoors. I'd packed a lunch, I had the diaper bag for a quick change, we had a ball and a ring-toss game. I was looking forward to it. By the time I arrived near the swings and slide, there were a dozen moms, strollers, and kids in the area. Whoopie! I was looking forward to a little parenting talk.

"I made our camp near the sandbox, smiled at the other parents, who happened to be all mothers, and asked which little ones were theirs. This part went well, although one mother moved herself to another area. I should have sensed right then that I was an intruder.

"Eventually there were two moms near me, watching the kids play together. After we introduced ourselves, I asked some dopey question about potty training. One woman patted my hand and said I should just leave it up to my wife. Here again was that mystique: only women can do certain things. When I said I was a single father, one mother took pity on me and said I could stop in and see what she was doing in this mysterious field.

"Late one afternoon I did. In fact she and I were in their bathroom looking at a newfangled musical potty chair. The kids were racing about, and we didn't hear her husband come home. When he cleared his throat at the bathroom door, she got all flustered. He put his arm on my shoulder and walked me downstairs. As he saw me out the door he said, 'Don't you bother my wife anymore!'

"He didn't even hear my explanation. Boy, was I ever humiliated! I realized that many men had delegated child care to women, and that a man just shouldn't be doing it. Also, I realized that many men didn't want any poor dumb fathers associating with their wives! And I realized that many women didn't really want any men in their little club. From then on, I asked my questions of the pediatrician or via long-distance, of my sister, or I just bungled along on my own. In many ways it has been a lonely journey."

5. *Answering questions about "Mama."*

What can Troy say about "Mama"? Trevor doesn't think of Tracy as "Mama" since he doesn't see her often and he was only five months old when she left. He once called her "pretty lady." On Trevor's toy shelf is a picture of the "pretty lady," Tracy.

When she is coming to visit, Troy instructs Trevor to give her a kiss, to be very good, and to have fun. He never says anything negative about her.

Sometime in the future Troy will have to share more information. Without putting down Tracy, he can tell Trevor about their school days, marriage, and how she gave birth to him. Troy is prepared to say that Tracy had a wonderful job that took her away from them, so Daddy had to take full charge. Further explanations as to why she isn't living with them can be left to Tracy.

Because so many youngsters live with one parent, usually the mother, Trevor may find a special prominence to be living with a father.

Troy often finds himself buying things for Trevor to, as he says, "make up to him for not having a mother." Troy now has a good income and can afford nice clothes, vacations to visit relatives, and renovating the old house.

Most women are not as fortunate when they are the prime custodian. A woman's income, alimony, and child support rarely provide for anything beyond the minimum requirements. This inequity of life-styles was one of the main complaints of women who took part in my survey.

However, nothing makes up for love, and Troy certainly gives a lot of that to Trevor.

❖ ❖ ❖

While Troy has the opportunity to actually raise his son, fathers everywhere are missing out on their children's growing up years. One father told me: "There are no rights for noncustodial fathers. We give the money, we get little in return." These fathers miss the tragedies and triumphs of family life, the companionship of a wife and children.

Although there are many fathers who want to abdicate the nitty-gritty of parenting, there are many others who have a genuine interest in their children's day-to-day well-being. What can be done to help them? They sincerely believe that they have skills that would benefit a child. One father somewhat solved this by becoming his son's Little League coach. He sees him twice weekly and has unstructured time with him after the weekly game.

But this solution is no help to a father I know who lives across the country from his child. His plan includes weekly calls and letters, gifts for many occasions, and a two-week yearly visit. "This is nothing," he says sadly. "I'm just an occasional visitor in her life."

KEYS FOR SUCCESS

Fathers will be much happier and a lot more influential in their children's lives if they educate themselves about parenting and then work to put that education into practice. This is not easy, but it is possible.

Many single parents in my survey were fathers, but most did not have primary custody of their children. Most felt keen pain over the separation, and a few cried out for better custody laws, citing the success of divided custody.

At the same time these fathers expressed difficulty in learning parenting skills. Certainly books are a help, but hands-on experience is better. One said, "To really be an effective parent, you have to know your child deeply. You can't do this without sufficient time together." Togetherness at all costs is another key to success.

For the best solution, parents should put aside their animosities and work out a plan that gives both parents prime time with their children. This may require special scheduling of work time and leisure time. A regular routine—whether it is alternate weeks, weekends, or long vacation periods—needs to be agreed on sooner rather than later.

Troy's keys to success include a fierce determination to raise his own child and a strong sense of family love. Certainly he needs to start creating a life for himself, and one that includes both men and women friends. In many ways he was still a child when he married and became a father. He was rushed into responsibilities he wasn't prepared for. He'd never even held a baby before Trevor was born.

Women have long been the traditional caregivers. Now men are learning that there is no mystery to being a good parent. It just takes a bit more work for them to catch up. But they will.

CHAPTER FIVE

"My Biological Clock Was Running Out"

The story of one woman's journey into parenthood

FIVE WOMEN SAT AROUND THE sidewalk restaurant table in sunny Tucson, drinking coffee and talking comfortably. As they introduced themselves to me, I could see that they were confident about themselves and their individual lives. Their links to one another went back to college or earlier jobs and their current careers were quite varied. They called themselves the BC Club—meaning "biological clock."

It was an interesting array of careers: a legal secretary, an insurance salesperson, a freelance writer, a computer troubleshooter, and an employee of the telephone company who actually climbed poles to make repairs.

Outwardly, they didn't have much in common aside from enjoying good conversation about every topic imaginable. Another thing they had in common was that not one of them was married but each one wanted to have children. My friend Linda, who had invited me to that gathering, was the computer expert.

Now seven years had passed since I first attended this week-end get-together. Through the years I had kept in touch with Linda and occasionally asked about the others. Now she shared with me what had happened in the intervening years.

She began by saying that the members of the BC Club could accomplish more in one Saturday-morning coffee session than most people could in a week. These women had not merely hoped to become mothers; they began methodically investigating every possible avenue, and they knew one another well enough that they freely discussed each option.

And so today, my friend Linda summarized their research for me but was quick to explain that they had acquired a big fat file of information on each topic. Seven years ago they had realized it was time for action. They were all "thirty-something," and there were few prospects for marriage.

It wasn't as if they hadn't been asked. Most of them had been in serious relationships; one had lived with a boyfriend for five years, two had been engaged. They were attractive, productive women with good minds.

"That's one of the problems," said Linda. "I know people say that many men are intimidated by smart women. But we weren't show-offs, we just didn't think it honest to play dumb or coy just to get a man. Gradually the pool of available men dwindled, and many could be ruled out for good reasons."

"What are good reasons?" I asked. She laughed and said, "Well, one of the group dated a guy for two months, and then he confessed he was gay and was just trying to see if he could make it as a heterosexual. And then there are the married men just looking for extracurricular fun, and the religious fanatics who only want to save you by converting you to their brand of religion. In addition there are many men who just don't have any personality. Now we were not looking for movie stars or astrophysicists; we were each just looking for a sincere, loving man who would enjoy spending a lifetime in a family."

Linda explained how they had started researching their options. "We each chose to become an expert in one field. Meghan, the legal secretary, found out about sperm banks. Sybil, the one in insurance, investigated in vitro fertilization. Eve, the freelancer, considered what it would be like to marry just to have a child, and then perhaps divorce the guy.

"Debbie's topic was called 'hire a dad.' The group humorously renamed it 'hire a stud.' In her telephone company work she found that a lot of macho males would be happy to have a sexual fling with a gal as long as there was no permanent commitment. Her idea was to pick someone intelligent with average good looks and agree to make a baby together—but there would be no rights for the father, no contact, no support. She investigated the legalities of this as we each did on our separate subjects.

"My area was adoption. I found out immediately that most adoptions in the United States would take a very long time—averaging almost three years—if a healthy Caucasian infant was wanted. Older children, children with mental and physical problems, or children of African-American descent would be easier to adopt. We all knew that being a single parent would be a lot of work with an average baby, and most felt that they wouldn't be able to handle the additional problems of a child with a handicap. This may sound selfish, but we knew our limits. And most of the group felt they wanted to experience motherhood with a baby as near to birth as possible.

"It was then I began to investigate overseas adoptions. What a hassle! The time involved! The costs! I can tell you that in some cases you'd have to travel to the country and stay up to a month—that would eat up all your vacation or sick leave. And talking with parents who'd done it, I found that there was a mountain of bureaucratic stumbling blocks—and on top of that, you're usually dealing in a foreign language. The costs—to the adoption agency and the country involved, plus all the travel and legal costs—humongous! Most of us didn't have big savings accounts. We'd have to spend everything we had, and we'd be starting single parenting at ground zero financially.

"We seriously considered one more option: remaining childless. Somehow that didn't seem right for me. I wasn't trying to 'have it all' but I did want to have more. Also, there was the pressure of friends who kept pushing me to get married. They meant well and fixed me up with single men they knew, but nothing happened.

"I'd been raised as an only child of very religious parents who believed in a correct order for doing things. And having a baby only came *after* getting married. Sure, I'd love to be married, but only to someone I loved.

"So in the seven years since our Saturday morning coffee club started this project, we kept in touch for the first few years. Now we've gone our separate ways and meet only occasionally.

"Debbie married a telephone company supervisor and had triplets she named for AT&T—Alex, Tom, and Ted. I don't think she's wildly in love with her husband and it's a financial struggle, but I think they'll stay together because those little guys are really a handful.

"Sybil, the one in insurance, is a very cautious person. She's still looking around as she approaches age forty. I think she's gotten more into creature comforts and material possessions than parenting. I doubt she'll ever be a mom.

"Eve, the freelancer, is the free spirit of the group. She has a toddler. Although we were quite open in the past, she's kept us guessing as to what her method was—a visit to a sperm bank or 'hire a dad.' I don't see her much anymore.

"Neither Meghan nor I ever married, but we opted for adoption. I guess she's more noble than I am as she adopted an eleven-year-old handicapped child. Of all of us, she has the biggest income, so she's able to provide good treatment and special care. We're good friends, and so I see the day-by-day progress those two are making."

Later, we were sitting on Linda's deck on a breezy day in Tucson. The townhouses had a common green with swings and slides, and we watched the children play as we talked. Linda pointed out a chubby four-year-old wearing a big sunbonnet.

"That's my Annie," she said proudly. "What a dynamo!" Annie waved, blew a kiss our direction, and raced to the top of the slide again.

I asked Linda how she happened to decide on adoption. Linda replied, "It was a process of elimination. I'm too honest to marry some guy I didn't love and then maybe divorce him after the baby was born. Besides, I couldn't find any likely prospects for a wedding.

"The idea of having a friend of mine father the baby and then take a hands-off position scared me a little. The father would always be around and I wanted no strings on this child. I know a woman who made this arrangement. The man was married to someone else at the time but promised to start a trust fund for the baby. Sure, he said he was going to get a divorce. All of that turned out to be baloney and caused her a lot of heartache. I couldn't go through that—it would be worse than divorce.

"Of course, the sperm bank method would be anonymous. You can pick the donor's occupation, race and nationality, education, color of eyes, and all sorts of other things. But that seemed so clinical. And I'll have to admit I wasn't that interested in going through pregnancy at my age and with my job.

"So that left adoption. I connected with a respected adoption agency—well, actually two agencies—but I chased many dead ends there. First, I was going to go to Hungary and bring back several children for other worthy adoptive parents. Then I found that prostitutes there were 'manufacturing' kids for export, and many babies had serious health problems. Some children had been institutionalized for so long that it was doubtful the effects could be overcome. All that turned me off.

"Next I looked into Korean babies, but that country would only deal with married couples. Then I considered China, but other adoptive parents gave me horror stories of the orphanages and the incredibly endless red tape. So I investigated Colombia; but many of the birth parents were into drugs, and their babies were born horribly addicted. Finally I looked right across the border, and that's where I found Annie."

We walked down to the play area and Annie ran into Linda's arms. She smiled and kissed her mama, and even gave my knees a hug. "Time for juice!" she announced emphatically.

Sitting on the deck and eyeing the other children on the slide, she gulped down the apple juice and went right back to play. We sat at the table on the deck, watching and talking.

"It wasn't an easy decision. First, I wondered what people would think. Then I realized that was a foolish diversion. People who knew me would know how much I wanted a child, and they'd know I'd do my best to be a good mother. People who would be critical just wouldn't be my close friends, so the criticism wouldn't be valid.

"Then there were my folks. Right away they wanted to know what would happen if 'Mr. Right' came along and maybe didn't want to be a father to a Mexican child. I had the answer for that one: if he didn't like my child, he wasn't 'Mr. Right.'

"Eighteen months passed following my first application— months filled with paperwork, translations, approvals, legal work, and finally the adoption. Gradually my parents got actively involved in my project, encouraging me to hang in there and get this child. They helped in many ways, but their moral support was the best.

"At one point, after all the paperwork seemed complete and I'd gone to Mexico City, where I met and fell in love with my baby, the question of my being single came up—again. That had been settled long before, but some government official began to object. It was a time of lots of tears and frustration. It took two more weeks of my vacation time, and with a friend to translate for me, we traveled to another city to speak with the man who stood between me and my child. We talked and talked, and he kept shaking his head. Then suddenly he shook my hand. Annie was mine!

"Adjusting to home life with a twenty-month-old baby took a little doing. Friends helped me those first weeks—bringing me equipment I needed, giving me a baby shower, dropping off casseroles, offering to care for her at times when I was extremely tired.

"At the same time all this was going on, I borrowed some language tapes to bolster my two years of high school Spanish. I used my bath time and some of my car travel time to learn. I wanted to raise Annie to be bilingual, and it has turned out to be fun. But it was really frustrating at first. She'd shout at me in toddler Spanish and because I couldn't understand, I'd shout something back in English.

"That was when we started our 'word-a-day' plan. After a few months, we were learning many words each day—both Spanish words and English words. Now that she's almost five, we're each at ease in both languages."

I asked what was the most difficult part of being an adoptive mother. She didn't hesitate when she said, "Not having someone close to consult with. No one to talk it over. No one to 'spell' you. No one to get up in the night when the child cries out. But then, I've never had these perks, unlike married and then divorced mothers who had them and then had to learn to do without them. At least I never felt that something was taken away from me.

"I recognize that I have to work out my frustrations on my own. Business associates say I've developed a short temper and a sharp tongue. And I notice that when Annie tests me, I overreact. But I love her so much that I know I'll get calmer. But I don't think there's anything more trying to one's patience than a toddler.

"My current problem involves planning for Annie's care when the school day ends; and then the money for college, many years down the road, is always on my mind. It's a lot to do alone, and sometimes I just cry. But usually I'm upbeat about motherhood.

"I know I'm not doing enough about seeing that she has those all-important male role models. It's hard to connect with guys on a casual basis, and her day-care people are all female. My neighbors are grandparents with grandchildren living in Ohio who they only see about once a year. One of these grandkids is the same age as Annie, so they've taken on the role of proxy grandparents. That way they have a good idea about what their own grandchild is learning to do.

"Annie's day-care workers are a big help when I have to work overtime. She will start prekindergarten this year, and they may be willing to pick her up at two o'clock and care for her until I get home at six. That would be a big weight off my shoulders.

"One thing a single mother learns quickly: to be creative, to think ahead, to always think of the child first. There's no time off—or at least very little—when you've agreed to take good care of a child.

"Although I have told Annie the story of how we got to be a family, she doesn't understand it yet. She keeps asking where her daddy is. I tell her that her first mommy and daddy loved her so much but they couldn't care for her, so they let me be the mommy. She likes that, but then demands, 'Where is the daddy to go with *you*, mommy?' I know I have to figure out an answer to that!

"Among my current friends are both married and single parents. It isn't as strange to be a single parent now as it was a decade ago. Or maybe I've just sought out a number of single moms for friendship.

"People look at blonde me when I'm grocery shopping with Annie in the cart. They just smile at me in an approving way.

"You know, my aim wasn't totally a selfish one. Sure, I wanted a child, but I also wanted to save a child. I guess that's why I opted for foreign adoption. In my long search I learned of children with no future but hunger and poverty. I wanted to give a child a good life, a good education, and lots of love. I can do that.

"There are so many children out there. Children who have little hope for a good life. Children just waiting and waiting. This one was waiting for me."

Challenges

Because Linda had taken sufficient time to think through the ramifications of this biggest event in her life, she was prepared for parenthood. The classes, the book-reading, the foreign-language study she undertook following the adoption have further prepared her, and she's doing well. Looking ahead, these will be her challenges:

1. Giving Annie a full life with both male and female role models
2. Helping a child come to terms with abandonment
3. Reducing her own level of frustration as a single parent

Some Solutions

1. Giving Annie a full life with both male and female role models.

Linda's friends are a help, and teachers can also fill this need. I hope that somewhere in the near future there is a Hispanic family who will become friends with Linda and Annie.

The question of role models is one of the major problems of single parenting. Joining parenting groups, taking part in church activities and clubs can help. But having the time to nurture one or more role models doesn't fit Linda's schedule at present. Like many single mothers, she's extremely busy earning a living. She has no second income from a man or any child support payments to fall back on, so all her time is committed to her career and Annie's needs.

2. Helping a child come to terms with abandonment.

For some adopted children, the question is, "Did my birth parents love me?" When the birth parents are known, the answer is usually, "They loved you, but knew they couldn't care for you, so they gave you to us so that you could have a happy life."

However, more and more adoptive children have not been "given up" for adoption, but rather abandoned. This is the case with Annie. She was left on a street corner—no parental contact, no note of explanation, no clues.

While Annie is content at present with the answer, "They couldn't take care of you," she will want to know more as she gets older. Overcoming the feeling of being abandoned is difficult. Linda will want to emphasize the importance of Annie in her life, and Annie's own qualities that will build self-esteem.

Adopted children often feel more distressed about being given up by their birth parents than they show. It takes an intuitive parent to know what to say and how much to say. Ongoing reassurance is needed.

One adopted baby boy grew up hearing positive things about his birth mother who had died after childbirth. Thirty years later, after meeting the relatives of his birth mother, he happily told his adoptive parents, "You know, I'm surprised, she really *was* a good person!" The adoptive parents thought they'd covered that point many times already, but it often remains a question in the back of the adopted child's mind.

Research is beginning to uncover problems with children concerning their concepts about their birth parents. Adoptive parents often assume that when the adoption is final the subject is a closed book. For some, counseling is necessary. For some, more assurance and love will help overcome the sadness of being abandoned.

---

3. *Reducing her own level of frustration as a single parent.*

As Annie grows, she is going to do many things that will annoy Linda. Linda has a short fuse and needs to control her temper.

While she is never abusive to Annie, she admits she's a strident boss at the office. Probably some of her management techniques carry over to home and cause problems. After having lived alone, she needs to adjust to a child and the ways of children. Fostering within herself the childlike qualities of innocence, sweetness, and inquisitiveness should be foremost in Linda's parent/child relationship.

KEYS TO SUCCESS

Linda's many strengths and her desire to be a good mother will help her become successful. Her biggest advantage is that she was a "whole person" herself before she added Annie to her family. She has intelligence and self-confidence, plus increasingly solid parenting skills. She was also successful in choosing the right way in her situation to have a child. She had investigated all the options. And when she made a decision, she carefully followed through on each step, making sure that every aspect was absolutely detailed and legal. This careful attention is wise for her present peace of mind. It also ensures that there won't be any unpleasant legal surprises in the future.

Her decision to raise Annie bilingually is admirable. So many adoptive parents ignore a child's roots. I know a wise adoptive mother who retained her daughter's Chinese name as a middle name. She also brought from China a variety of photos and picture books of the child's home territory. Although money was scarce as she prepared to leave China, the mother purchased toys, fabrics, and porcelains. These items will be an important part of the baby's heritage.

Linda plans to visit Mexico with her daughter next summer, and she is confident that they'll have a wonderful time together.

Yes, there are so many children, just waiting and waiting.

CHAPTER SIX

"Look at Me, Up and Off Welfare!"

A courageous, can-do woman triumphs over the system

AS IF THEY HAD BEEN INVITED to a banquet, the birds attacked the crusts of bread. Josie and I were sitting on a bench in the park, eating sandwiches and grapes. It was a beautiful and cool sanctuary in an otherwise scorching Texas city.

Josie tossed out another crust and said, "Twenty years ago I couldn't have afforded to share even a crust with those birds. We ate every crust and licked every bowl clean. It was hard to teach my kids good manners when we had to scrape the last little bit out of every dish. Oh, I know there are hungry people today, but even back then we really knew hunger firsthand.

"At that time, we lived on the second floor of a two-story frame house—my husband, me, three kids, and a fat cat that had just sort of moved in. The cat ate the best since there were plenty of mice around. We use the nice word *mice* nowadays, but then we knew they were rats."

Josie leaned forward thoughtfully and continued. "You

asked how I got into this mess. I was born in Mississippi and the first smart thing I ever did was to leave that little town. If I'd stayed I would have continued sitting around, having babies, trying to live off a miserable piece of land. I'd probably be dead by now."

I asked how she got from Mississippi to Texas. She answered, "The way God meant us to travel—on our own two feet, using our own good sense. Oh, there were some rides along the way, but mostly our little group walked along back roads, thinking that the further west we got, the better it would be. But, when we arrived in this city, we found that it was the same thing all over again. The blacks were at the bottom—the absolute bottom for jobs, housing, food, and schooling.

"I'd finished high school so I got a job at that Army base near here. At least the place was air-conditioned. A handsome corporal sweet-talked me into going out with him and we went to a drive-in movie on our first date."

Josie gave me a wicked grin and continued, "That first date kinda rushed things along and in three months we were married. It probably wasn't love, just wanting someone to be with. A year later Joseph Junior was born.

"They were fighting a war in Vietnam, and we lived under the stress of his going away. When he finally left, I was pregnant again; this time it was a girl. We liked Bible names and called her Ruth. Left without husbands, all the gals got friendly and took care of one another's babies. Life was about as simple as it could get.

"Then Big Joe came home. Although he had suffered a serious leg wound, in a while he was okay physically. But he was *never* the same in his mind. He didn't do much—just sat around and watched TV while I kept my job at the base. A year later, Naomi was born. I could see that I wasn't financially much better off having a job. At that time there was a little hope in Texas for folks like us.

"The kids really got to Joe. Actually, everything got to him. Especially when he and the Army parted company over his fighting with his buddies. This meant we moved off the base to an old house where we had the second floor to ourselves. The kitchen was downstairs so I cooked there and carried all the food up. Big Joe kept saying he was going to get a job, but for the first months he stayed home and watched the kids as I continued to work at the base. We were fast using up the money he got when he left the Army.

"One day I came home from work and the kids were there by themselves. Ruth had taken a screen off the second floor window and was waving at me as I came up the walk. In charge was four-year-old Joe Junior, supposedly taking care of a two-year-old and a baby. All he said was, 'I know how to do, Mama!' And bless him, he did. He had a rope around Ruthie's waist, and it was tied to the bed! I asked him if his daddy had gone down to a store, but he shook his head. Nothing was missing in the place—Joe's clothes were there—only his favorite radio was gone.

"We waited supper on him that night, and the next night, and the next. Then I went to the police and told them what had happened, and they didn't do anything; they didn't even write down my name. Now without Big Joe to watch the kids, I couldn't go to work, and we were fast running out of food and money.

"By the time I realized that Big Joe was gone for real, we had four dollars and thirty-nine cents left. Fortunately we'd been churchgoers, and so I got some food and clothes there. Then some friends were moving away, and they gave us everything that didn't fit in their car. I didn't know how to do things proper; but I'd heard about welfare, and I decided this was what I needed.

"Except they wouldn't give it to me because I didn't know where Joe was. Over and over I tried to explain it all. Nothing happened. We lived on handouts for six months until I finally began to get some welfare money. I don't know how they expected me to live on that, pay someone to watch the kids, get some decent clothes, and look for a job! But I couldn't argue because I was afraid they'd take away even the temporary funds.

"One thing the folks who'd moved away gave us was an old red wagon—the kind kids love. It became my transportation. To look for a job, I'd borrow a dress, shoes, hat, and handbag from a neighbor. She wore the outfit on alternate days when she went job hunting. It was funny when one restaurant guy said, 'Didn't I just tell you yesterday that we had no jobs?'

"I meant what I said about the wagon being my transportation. We lived on a hill, with all the businesses being down by the river. I'd get all dressed up to go looking, get in that wagon and coast for nine blocks, holding on to my handbag with one hand and my hat with the other. I had no hand left to steer. I only crashed once and that was into an ice cream truck. The ice cream man felt so bad for me that he gave me four popsicles and I dragged myself and the wagon right back up the hill so the kids could have the treats before they melted. It was a week before my bruises looked good enough for me to go out again. From then on, when I left to go job hunting, the kids always said, 'Get ice cream, Mama.'

"Other times when no one would watch the kids, I'd put them in the wagon and just park the wagon outside the store where I was looking for work. I threatened them good so they wouldn't get out of the wagon. By the way, that was one thing I guess I did right. I never beat my kids, but I made it clear how they were to behave. I taught them to be honest, to have respect, and to work hard.

"Eventually I got a job as a cook on the night shift at a diner. I could leave the kids asleep and the woman downstairs would check on them. It turned out I was pretty good—especially at sauces and gravies—and after two long years, I got a raise. It wasn't much. Well, it was actually too much. Suddenly, the welfare folks said I was earning too much to still collect welfare. That was impossible, I thought, since I ended up with less money because of the tax deductions. I argued and pleaded, but the system won."

Lunch was over, the birds were stuffed with crusts, and we walked across the street to the porch of a small brick bungalow, complete with picket fence. Josie's smart dark suit and white chiffon blouse looked out of sync with this quaint house. I sat in a rocker, she in the swing, lazily gliding back and forth as she continued her story.

"Now came the big decision—was it worth having less money to be off welfare? No, I thought, and quit my job and stayed home with the little ones. Little Joe was in kindergarten by now so there were only two left at home. But you know, I felt rotten about myself. I had found that there was something I could do to earn a living and provide for my family, so I decided I'd better do it. Welfare may let some people live a lazy or—as they say nowadays—nonproductive life, but I wanted more.

"At first I couldn't get my same job back; but I was persistent, and when I finally did, I made this vow: I will never go on welfare again. I stayed with that restaurant for six years; and although we barely survived, at least I had some dignity and so did the kids. The restaurant manager occasionally let me take home some good food. We wore uniforms at work, and the owner paid for them. So, with this help we could just manage.

"By the time all the kids were in school, I was working days but still earning a few bucks above the poverty level. We desperately needed more income. Joe Junior got a paper route—that was good money except when folks didn't pay him on time or pretended they didn't get the paper and wouldn't pay him at all. Until I talked turkey to those cheapskates, he actually lost money some weeks.

"One day we saw a 'For Rent' sign on this house. The owner was moving to a retirement home, but he wanted to keep the place. It was more out in the country then, and he said we could have it for half the money if we'd care for his two horses, which were in a barn that was way out at the back of the property. He would pay for the horses' feed.

"Caring for the old horses became Ruth's contribution to the family. How she loved them! The cats had long since run away to some place that had tastier mice, so the horses became our pets. The kids felt rich, riding them in circles around the yard. Ruth would have brought those horses inside the house if I'd have let her.

"Naomi was only five at the time, but she had her work, too. I taught her how to fold the laundry at the laundromat while I sat by, reading books. In fact, every spare minute I had was spent with my nose in a book—any book I could get my hands on. Soon I decided I was smart enough to take some night classes. For years, I was gone two nights a week but a girl up the street watched the kids until Joe Junior was twelve. Then I paid him twenty-five cents a night to babysit the girls.

"About then we discovered the art of bartering. We grew some vegetables, mainly tomatoes and beans, and we'd cart them to a local store which sold them. In exchange we got the other foods we needed. I found we could live on a food budget of five dollars a week!

"By the time Joe started high school, I got brave enough to take evening classes at the nearby junior college. All four of us would do our homework together. I was the slowest, and sometimes I was too sleepy to see the pages, but I worked at it a little at a time and soon I was getting good grades. The kids loved to check my report cards!

"When the owner of this house died, he left it to a church nearby. They wanted to sell it and have the money. I figured that if I quit night school and took a second job, I could buy the house with no down payment but instead pay a certain amount every month. I talked it over with the kids and each decided to contribute some of their earnings to payments on the house. And so the church accepted my terms and was happy to have the steady money.

"It was scary to sign all those papers, but we did it together. Even Naomi wanted to help by cleaning the Sunday school at the church. They didn't think she could do it, but she did a good job. I'd taught her how to clean real good."

Josie invited me inside. The house was solidly built and quite spacious, and I especially noticed the beautifully upholstered sofa and chairs. She said, "Buying this house was a turning point. We made a list of what each of us could do to improve it. I never bugged the kids. If they wanted to paint, they painted. If they wanted to polish the floors, fine.

"Then one day a year or so later, a real estate man called and asked if we'd be willing to sell the back half of the property. It was already zoned commercial, and an upholstery shop wanted to convert the barn to a workshop. This meant we had to sell the horses, but Ruth was busy with school now, and ready to part with them. With the money from the sale of the back lot and the horses, we felt wealthy!

"Joe was graduating from high school later that year. Without any prompting from me, the girls suggested that the money go for a college education for him. He suggested that it be divided among the three of them, so that they could all have some money for schooling.

"So, when Joe was accepted at a college about fifty miles from here, we really celebrated. He got a part-time job in the refectory at the school, and a second job in the library. That gave him enough money for his first car—it was old but it usually ran. I was so proud to have a real collegiate in the family.

"At that point, I could afford to go back to night classes. Ruth got an after-school job at the upholstery shop. That's how we have such nice furniture—she redid every piece in her free time, with remnants the shop let her have. Then, the next year, she went off to the same school as Joe, majoring in fabric design. She and Joe would come home weekends to see Naomi and me.

"Now, there was just the two of us. I was now an assistant chef, but the work had become pretty dull. That's not unusual after about ten years of stirring the same stuff! Still, I had no proven skills and couldn't afford to quit. The manager wanted to keep me, so he let me do the menu planning for the diner and for his second restaurant. I liked this challenge and decided I'd take more advanced courses in food handling and nutrition. Another turning point.

"Soon it was time for Naomi to think about her career. She chose to go to school here, the same four-year college I attend. Now I had extra time to study plus another raise, so I kept going, taking courses as I could. I really enjoy the nutrition field. It's been four years now, and Naomi graduates this month."

Josie stops, looks at me and smiles for the first time. Then she says with a tilt of her head, "Guess what? I'm gonna graduate with her!"

Josie's mood became serious again and she added, "I wonder what Big Joe would think of his three children and wife, all with college degrees!"

Challenges

While most of Josie's major problems are behind her, she still has some challenges ahead that include:

1. Making a good career for herself
2. Keeping a feeling of family togetherness
3. Continuing to grow herself
4. Finding time to help others

Some Solutions

1. Making a good career for herself.

Now that she has her college degree, Josie is no longer content with her present restaurant job. However, she feels that there are not many career opportunities for African American women in her city. There is no real reason to stay in this area since two of her children now live and work in other cities, and Naomi will be leaving home soon.

She hasn't traveled much in her life, and it would be good for her to take a vacation and drive to some pre-selected nearby cities where she might enjoy living and where there are better job opportunities.

Because she married young and needs to work another twenty years or more, she should consider a move now that she's sufficiently educated to step up in her profession.

She fears that her race and her sex are roadblocks to success. In her work, at college, and in talking with friends, she's felt the barriers of racism and sexism. At present she is letting these fears keep her safely where she is, even though this means stifling her talent.

2. *Keeping a feeling of family togetherness.*

While her children are very important to her, she has been so busy working and going to school, that she hasn't had time to build many good family memories and traditions. Now that Joe and Ruth are married and have families, Josie longs for more togetherness. They live only a hundred miles away and with some encouragement, she could do more to bring them all together. She says "telephoning is expensive," but she doesn't take the time to write, either.

She fears she is "losing" her children now that they no longer need her encouragement. But she has no reason to feel that way since she admits that they extend invitations to her for vacations and holidays. She seems reticent, though, to respond with invitations for *them* to visit her. She says her neighborhood has become quite commercial, and she really needs to find a more suitable place to live. When she finally lives alone, Josie will really see the need for family ties. Now is the time to strengthen them.

3. *Continuing to grow herself.*

For the past several decades, Josie hasn't had much time for her own personal development, beyond her educational aims. So wrapped up in children, work and schooling, she has made few friends on her own.

One thing she has going for herself is a deep devotion to her religion. She enjoys the service at a nearby church. Although it offers many opportunities for making friends and participating in activities, she keeps putting off making the connection.

A life of fighting her way up has made her possessive of her private time, and she now needs to broaden her life horizons. The time formerly spent with the children or earning her degree could now be used to find new and exciting things to do. She holds herself back from new experiences, being content in the familiar.

---

4. *Finding time to help others.*

It is strange to say that a woman who has given so much to her children is actually selfish in some ways. She proudly says, "I did it all by myself," and she is quick to add that others should do the same. She says that everyone has to find a way out of the wasteland of poverty, ignorance, and racism. Certainly there must first be a desire to leave that wasteland, but there's nothing sinful about giving or accepting a helping hand. Sometimes that makes all the difference.

If she honestly looked back at her life, she would see that there were helping hands for her throughout the years. In her city are many organizations that could now channel her courage and determination in ways that would help others triumph over "the system."

KEYS TO SUCCESS

The realization that welfare was not an acceptable long-term way of life set Josie on the right track. Finding a niche in busi-

CHAPTER SEVEN

"Suddenly I Knew This Child Needed Me"

A mother recalls the terror of her own abusive youth and saves a child

BEING A PARENT WAS NEVER high on Denice's list of priorities. She was an only child, so she had no experience with siblings. The little children in her neighborhood were okay but nothing special. She had a part-time job in a department store during high school, so she didn't babysit. In college she went around with other women whose major aim was a good career and not necessarily marriage and motherhood.

So she was a bit surprised at herself when she was suddenly rocketed into parenthood, and single parenting at that!

We first met in her purchasing office which was well furnished and orderly. She seemed unruffled by the phone calls and drop-ins that interrupted our conversation.

Waving a hand around her office she said, "This may look like I'm important and well paid, but I'm not. I'm just barely making it. In fact, I have another job, a business of my own that takes some evening and weekend hours: I do computer writing for others. But I especially like my job here."

She picked up a silver-framed picture and showed it to me. "That's Monica. She's my real life." The child had honey-colored hair, blue eyes, and a radiant smile just like her mother.

She went on: "I don't think the life of a single mother is what my parents had in mind for me. As an only child I was treated like a princess. The kids next door always said I was so lucky. I'll tell you more about one of them later.

"My parents were overjoyed that I did well in school. My mother was a grade-school teacher—in fact she still is—and my dad was a high school principal until he retired recently. So I had lots of encouragement to excel, to get my undergraduate degree at a good college, and then to get an advanced degree.

"Certainly I gave some thought to marriage and dated a few men, one quite seriously. One by one, they marched through my life and then married someone else. So when I passed the big three-zero, I decided that I'd better pay stricter attention to my work, because marriage was probably not going to be the highlight of my life."

She smiled. "But as much as I like my management duties, I've found something better, and it's being a mother. But let me tell you more in the privacy of my living room."

So we adjourned to Denice's home, a comfortable split-level in the suburbs of a city in the Pacific Northwest. Pine trees fringed the large yard and rhododendrons punctuated the greenery with vibrant spots of color. The living room had Berber carpet and tweedy upholstery, watercolors on the walls, plus three handsome cats who sat perched on the chair backs suspiciously watching me.

"You may not believe this part, and it still seems so strange to me how it all happened. I wasn't looking for a child, yet a child found me. It began one Sunday after church. I had just moved to a good-sized apartment of my own and asked my parents to come by for some lunch.

"They said they couldn't because they were helping a young woman that they had known from the high school. I'd known her too, a quiet loner named Bonnie. Bonnie had just left her husband, escaping with her toddler to the safety of my folks' house. She was really taking advantage of them: eating everything in sight, watching their TV day and night, using their car and phone, taking over the den for herself and her child—just making herself at home without helping at all.

"Something had to happen as my folks were getting frantic with suppressed anger. So when I stopped by my folks' house a few days later, I foolishly asked Bonnie if she wanted to move in with me until she got on her feet. She shrugged her shoulders but agreed. So there she was, living with me—trashing *my* house and eating *my* food. When I suggested an inexpensive daycare facility for her baby so she could look for a job, she just shrugged her shoulders again.

"It was evident that Bonnie was still under Clint's spell. After I'd met him, I thought he should be called Clyde since these two reminded me of the notorious 'Bonnie and Clyde' duo. I'm not a prude by any means, but this guy was up to no good. He'd come by half-drunk and whisk Bonnie out, just leaving two-year-old Monica with me. He didn't seem to care about his daughter at all.

"Now Monica was a charmer—the kind that smiled shyly, tossed her blonde curls, climbed into your lap, and then baby-talked a request you couldn't deny. As time passed, Monica was left with me for days, then weeks, then months. I got someone to care for her while I worked, and I tried not to fall in love with her, but I did.

"One day the year she was almost four, Monica asked if she could call me mommy. Of course I said 'yes,' but I was thinking with my heart, not my head. Up to that time, I was like an aunt, and I tried to hold her at arm's length, but now we began to function like a family. I had no chance to really think through the relationship. And worse yet, I didn't have any background in raising a child—just what I learned 'on the job.'

"So I stumbled along, falling more in love with her as each day passed. Then, out of nowhere, Bonnie reappeared one day after nearly a year's absence. I grew cold with fear that she'd take Monica away from me. But Bonnie hadn't come for the child. She wanted to collect some clothes she'd left behind. As she raced through the house, she suddenly asked if I'd like legal custody of Monica. Without a second thought, I accepted. So that's how we became a family." Denice sighed deeply. There were steps in the hall.

It was Monica, home from school, a tall twelve-year-old who looked so much like Denice that it was hard to believe that they weren't blood relatives. Shyly, Monica brought us juice and cookies and then left for a friend's home down the street, saying they were going to listen to some new CDs. Denice shook her head as she left.

After a pause, she continued, "Now comes the bad part. That very day, when Bonnie was packing up and Monica was in preschool, Bonnie told me why she had left Clint. She and Clint had a one-room apartment in town, and one day she came home unexpectedly and found him sexually abusing Monica. Imagine doing that to a two-year-old!"

We both sat quietly, Denice crying, me trying to be professional but on the verge of tears.

Denice continued, "I then put a lot of things together and realized that this had been going on for some time. I'd noticed things whenever they'd come in town and take Monica to their apartment for a few days. When they'd bring her back she was always extremely quiet and would sometimes have crying spells. Bonnie admitted that the abuse was why she had originally run away to my parents' home.

"I asked why she had gone back to Clint. She gave that familiar shrug and said that it was because of drugs—using them, abusing them, selling them. I was stunned when she asked if I knew she'd had a second little girl, born during the past months they'd been away. She admitted she was now going to move away with that baby, giving Monica to me. To her, it was most important to be near Clint, who was serving time in prison."

Denice smiled through her tears. "So here I am, seven years later, working my way through all this with Monica."

She stood up and walked around the room. "And so I've had Monica in counseling all these years. She is still afraid of tall men who look similar to Clint. And I'm also getting help for myself. You see, I too was an abused child."

Surprised at this latest revelation, I wondered how this could be, since she was a carefully raised only child of two educators. She stared out the window as I asked what she remembered.

She answered sadly, "Oh, all of it. I was about five years old. My folks always let the neighbor boy babysit when they had to go out. He was about fifteen and everyone in the neighborhood called him 'a good kid.' That was a laugh. He hardly waited for the car to leave the driveway before he started touching me. Because I always cried, he told me he'd blow up our whole house during the night if I ever said anything to anyone about our 'games.'

"The 'games' went on until he enlisted in the Army. I couldn't tell my parents, I was so afraid of him and ashamed and embarrassed for myself. I thought it was my fault. So I kept it to myself until I told a college roommate. She was understanding and encouraged me to get counseling. I've had counseling off and on for almost twenty years now."

Denice changed the subject and we talked about how she is continually learning new parenting skills. She admits she might not have gone into this had she known what was ahead. But she adds quickly that she is totally committed to being a good mother to Monica. At this point Monica returned to practice for her piano lesson, but first she talked with me.

Monica began brightly. "God put Mother and me together. We were meant to be a family. And we look alike. And we like music. And we LOVE cats. Because the cats are always rushin' around, we gave them Russian names. That's Yuri, and that's Boris, and that's Natasha," she said, pointing to the trio who leaped down from their perches and raced into the kitchen.

To a background of acceptable piano practice, Denice told me about their family life.

"It's simple, it's child-oriented, it's full of love. What we have is each other. My parents do what they can to help. Monica and I have friends from church and other groups, but we do most everything together when I'm not at work or Monica in school.

"I help out at Girl Scouts when I can, I listen to her piano lessons, we shop together, we even do our paperwork together. After dinner, I sit at the computer and she tries to get through her homework. Although her achievement-test scores are high, her report cards don't show it. The teachers say she just doesn't pay attention. They've started to label her as a slow learner. That's scary."

She then moves on to happier subjects. They observe a special tradition on Tuesdays. It is called "No TV Night." They have a special supper in the living room, then they read together, sometimes on their own, sometimes to each other.

Another tradition is Friday night supper at Grandma and Grandpa's. These grandparents truly love Monica and enjoy taking her to the zoo, museums and movies, and for hikes up a nearby mountain to play in the snow.

Denice then reveals that her daughter worries about family finances, an unusual concern for a preteen! She thinks that if they run out of money, they'll be separated and she'll be sent back to her birth mother. Although they've talked about the importance of not *wasting* money, Denice has never been able to help Monica enjoy buying things. Unlike most kids, she's never wanted to go to the toy store. She asks if her Christmas gifts are things they can afford. Recently, when she was asked to join the school band, she said she didn't want to because the instruments would be too expensive.

The piano practice ends. Monica comes over and puts her arms around her mother and asks, "Did I do better?" Denice reassures her and kisses her forehead several times.

Challenges

Denice is glad she is providing a stable life for Monica. It hasn't been easy. Monica fears for their relationship; she doesn't want to be abandoned again. These are Denice's challenges:

1. Overcoming the effects of abuse—against both child and mother
2. Learning parenting skills for the teen years ahead
3. Helping her daughter do better in school
4. Giving her daughter self-confidence and "loosing" her to experience things on her own
5. Working out a budget that can provide necessities, but also some extras

Some Solutions

1. *Overcoming the effects of abuse—against both child and mother.*

One can't change the horrors of the past. What happened, happened. But one can understand that the abuse was someone else's degenerate behavior. Hence, it shouldn't be permitted to have a life of its own, continue to tear apart the lives of innocent people. Denice is not to blame. Monica is not to blame.

While Denice is coming to this conclusion after years of counseling, Monica is not yet ready to give up the past. In fact she will not even discuss the abuse with Denice, saying it is "too gross," and if she tells about it, her precious mama will not want her anymore. Denice is reassuring, but she realizes how fragile her daughter is.

A few years ago, Monica's father called to say he was out of prison and wanted to see his daughter. Denice asked him if he was ready to pay child support. There was a long silence and then a click at the end of the line. He never tried to visit and he never telephoned again.

For a child, Monica expresses much anger toward her birth parents and those grandparents—all of whom have abandoned her. Now she needs reassurance that Denice will never let her return to that life. Monica needs to let the anger go as part of a past that will not return.

While Denice would like to adopt Monica formally, she doesn't want to upset the legal custody arrangements at the present time. She doesn't want to have anything to do with the abusers, which would be necessary if the matter went to court.

She's hoping to wait it out until Monica is old enough to legally choose for herself.

It is hard to keep confronting a problem that doesn't seem to budge. But this specter of abuse will continue to haunt this household until it is seen to be a phantom and is tossed out as powerless. The problem with abuse is that it makes the abused see many things from the standpoint of *victim*. It batters the self-esteem of both a child and an adult. Only by recognizing the strength of character that this mother and child really have, will they be able to put the abuse aside and go on with productive lives.

---

2. Learning parenting skills for the teen years ahead.

While Denice says she "backed" into parenting, she is doing a good job. However, you can go just so far on instinct. She needs to make friends with parents of children who are Monica's age so that she can talk about the present and future. Reading books or listening to tapes on parenting will help, too. Denice is a caring person, but she must learn more parenting skills.

Monica spends many afternoons at the home of a friend—a friend with two parents who work. Denice wonders if these opportunities for togetherness have led to sex exploration, but she doesn't know how to broach the subject without sounding suspicious. Certainly talk with the other family would be helpful. And it's time to set some rules—and actually write them down—on teen behavior. A child with low self-esteem is often prone to trying dangerous new things.

With the teenage years ahead, Denice should fortify herself with information on dating, drugs, alcohol abuse, premarital sex, AIDS, and all the temptations Monica will face. The close mother-daughter relationship is in her favor now. This is an important time to start a dialogue on these topics.

3. *Helping her daughter do better in school.*

It's hard for a mother who had a 4.0 average in college to raise a child who doesn't excel and seems disinterested in learning. Fortunately the teachers are helping Monica tackle the problem of attention deficiency. At home, Denice is teaching good study habits and helping Monica complete tasks.

Monica once said that she didn't like to compete in school because that got attention and she didn't want to be noticed. Denice could encourage her daughter to compete against herself—against her past test scores and grades. Monica's successes at home will give her feeling of self-worth a boost so that she won't mind being noticed occasionally.

It is evident that Monica wants to excel in piano and in band. The practice and mastery of these musical skills could then be transferred to academics. Learning to do quality schoolwork is important now, before the high school years begin. Denice is very low-key at home and needs to transfer some of her own office management dynamics to the home front. Encouragement ahead of time, and praise afterward for the smallest successes, will help.

One of Monica's saddest questions was, "If I don't do well in school, will you give me back?" Denice regularly affirms her commitment to be a mother forever, but Monica still worries. Having been abandoned once makes her think it could happen again.

4. *Giving her daughter self-confidence and "loosing" her to experience things on her own.*

You can't *give* a child self-confidence or self-esteem, but you can give a child the opportunities to experience these. Denice loves and protects Monica so much that Monica is socially immature for her age. She is old enough to bicycle to her music lesson on her own, rather than being driven by Denice. She should be given the responsibility of writing down her school and music assignments on her own, rather than having her mother do it, or call the school about it.

Monica is old enough for a clothing budget so that she can choose for herself what to wear. She needs to be given as many choices as possible: what to wear, what movie to see, what snack to have, whether to do homework before or after supper, what extracurricular activities to join.

Denice also needs to encourage Monica to have friends over. Denice is too much Monica's "best friend." Interaction with peers will do much for Monica's self-confidence in school and in other activities. She needs activities that will give her companionship (as opposed to the solitary life of a pianist), activities that bring her into social contact with other children. In six years or so, she will be leaving her protective nest, so some wing-testing needs to start now.

Sometimes Monica will fail. But more important, sometimes she will succeed on her own—and that's a valuable growing-up experience.

Like many youngsters, Monica wears glasses and is sensitive about her appearance. Kids can be cruel to fellow students who wear glasses, have different clothes, are slightly chubby, or come from a different background. A child should be taught to slough off insults, to accept some in good humor, and to entirely forget some. This hard assignment is better than accepting the insults as personal deficiencies and running away.

One thing that Monica wants is to get to know her younger sister. She is aware that her birth mother has a second child, a full sister to her. But her birth mother, out of a sense of guilt or meanness or because Monica knows the truth about Clint, prohibits this. This truly hurts Monica. As much as she'd like this connection, Denice is wise to protect her from the unsavory life of her birth parents.

Monica has worries about the future, especially when her mother dates (which is rarely). She wonders what will become of "mama and daughter" should a third person join the family. And Monica is still hesitant about her own close relationship with any man. Denice should engage in some "what-if" conversations with Monica, citing examples of how the family of two might be improved with a husband/dad.

Monica needs to feel the inclusive nature of family. Some good times with male role models, more than Friday nights with her grandfather, would be extremely beneficial. This would help her to overcome her hesitancy about men and increase her ability to trust again.

5. *Working out a budget that can provide necessities, but also some extras.*

Money, or lack of lots of it, makes problems for most single parents. Denice has never seen the necessity of a budget since things seem to "just work out." But Monica has latent fears about spending money, so she must have picked up this apprehension somewhere.

With a budget, Denice could show Monica just where their money goes. And she could include in the budget some discretionary funds that could be used for travel, clothes, a band instrument, or gifts. Of course we know Monica would like these things, but somehow she doesn't feel deserving. If she could actually see that there is money specifically put aside for certain things, she'd be more comfortable spending it.

It is rare that a child has this hesitancy about spending! But income and expense is a logical process, and Denice should not shield Monica from learning about it now.

Keys to Success

While Denice may not have known what she was getting into when she became the legal guardian for Monica, she is not a quitter. She knows she will always stand by this child. And she is determined to do her very best. They are a wonderful and caring twosome.

She says, "Think seriously before you adopt—I wouldn't do it differently, but I should have been aware of some of the difficulties. Going it alone isn't easy, especially in the middle of the night with a sick child. But the dawn always comes. My worst times are with Monica, but my best times are also with Monica."

At last, abuse in families is getting much-deserved attention, and Denice should be congratulated that she's tackling it. She says, "I have one advantage: there is no abuse in my own little family. We live our love."

It must be a continuing satisfaction for Denice to see the slow but steady progress of her daughter, a daughter she saved from an abusive childhood. Things may be difficult at times, but this courageous woman is proving daily that love conquers all.

CHAPTER EIGHT

"Could I Survive Alone with Three Teenagers?"

A dad shares the hard times he's had as a single parent

THE LIVING ROOM LOOKED AS if there had been an explosion. Rob and I had just walked in the front door of his two-story house, and we paused silently to look at the mess. He calmly picked up a whistle from the table and blew it. Suddenly from out of nowhere three T-shirt clad bodies appeared.

"Sorry, kids, I'm early, and we have a guest," he said pleasantly. Without argument or disgruntled looks, the games, magazines, clothes, and remnants of snacks were whisked away from floor, tables, sofas, and chairs. As each teenager sped by me, there was a handshake and a name given—Dino, Irena, Marco.

Dino plumped a sofa cushion and indicated it was now safe for me to sit there. In a moment Marco arrived with tomato juice and crackers on a tray. Then Irena announced they were all going upstairs to do homework. She said with a secretive grin, "We can fill you in on some of the gory details later. Just call us after Dad has told you all the good stuff."

113

Rob didn't seem at all flustered. "They're basically good kids, but they can sure mess up a house in a hurry!"

I'd met with Rob at his work place, an aeronautical firm in San Diego. Traveling in our separate cars, he led me from work to this house in the Hillcrest district. It was obvious we'd arrived ahead of schedule.

"It's nice living just fifteen minutes from work," he said. "I don't work overtime often because there's so much to manage here at home. But it wasn't always that way. In the old days I often didn't get home until eight or nine in the evening, figuring things were going okay here with my wife in charge. So, things seemed fine back then. Or, so I thought."

He told me how he ended up as single parent to three teens. "Sylvia and I had the usual marriage—a few arguments, a few detours, some good times with friends, season tickets for baseball, three kids in four years. It was a *good* life, but Sylvia wanted a *great* life. Three years ago, after fifteen years of marriage, she found it—or so she thought. I'm not sure.

"She was in her mid-thirties then and really into the body fitness thing. She didn't always have a job, but even when she did, she managed to work out a couple hours each day. Then this jock—about ten years her junior—took a special interest in her . . . a real special interest.

"I couldn't believe it when she asked for a divorce—right out of the blue, no hints, no discussions, just bam—the end. The kids couldn't understand it either. She'd been a good wife and mother, taking care of this house, bringing in some extra money from her beautician work, taking the kids to their sports events, clubs, and lessons, as well as cooking up quantities of hamburgers and enchiladas for all our friends. I had no idea she wasn't happy. Somehow, we'd never talked about happiness. Our conversation dealt with getting the things done that had to be done.

"I tried to stall on the divorce, saying we ought to think it over. She said there was nothing to think over: the kids were old enough to take care of themselves, and I should find someone else and have a life of my own. She made it clear that she still wanted to see the kids, but that I would be the prime caregiver.

"She used that word *caregiver*. I didn't know what it meant then, but I sure do now. I've been the chief caregiver for the past three years, and I could write a book on it. When I took over, the kids were eleven, thirteen, and fourteen—just moving into those busy, confusing teen years. Let me tell you, I know all about stuff that has initials: LSD, AIDS, SATs, NIMBY, even PMS. Now that I'm considered a professional by the guys at work, they come to me for advice. They don't write to 'Dear Abby,' they call for 'Dear Robby' when they're in trouble. And most of them have wives, and I don't."

I asked how he managed when he'd had little previous experience. He'd only been a father "in residence," and very little had rubbed off. He was happy to describe his on-the-job training.

"First, I had to get the kids' trust. They felt abandoned by their mom and worried I might decide they were too much trouble and up and leave, too.

"I found Marco crying in bed one night. He said no one loved him. Boy, I made sure after that these kids knew I loved them, and I wasn't going to give up on them. Now we might not have a lot of material stuff and not a lot of free time together, but we have a lot of love, and that was where we started.

"Once I was certain that they knew we'd stay together as a family, I appealed to them for cooperation. We sat around the dining table one Saturday night and wrote down everything that went on in this house—cooking, cleaning, laundry, yard work, repairs, school homework, television and Nintendo time, telephoning—a lot of that, planning for social times at the mall or school, going to sports practice and games. I looked at the long list all laid out before us in black and white, and I had a glimmer about why Sylvia wanted out!

"While I used to work overtime, now I stuck to a strict schedule and came home right after work. I don't think I had a night out by myself that first year. And the kids threw me some big problems: truancy at school, some pretty serious drug use, and bulimia—something I'd never even heard of. This parenting job was pretty challenging.

"There were days I thought of begging Sylvia to come back. Then, on one of her weekend drop-ins, I was startled to notice that she was pregnant. She and the jock were going to start this parenting thing all over again, so I knew I was on my own. I had no relatives nearby, and my friends were even less brilliant at fathering than I seemed to be. To top it all off, my job was a little shaky. There were some rumors of lay-offs, and I sure couldn't afford to lose my career at this point. After all, I had three other mouths to feed, and no wife to bring in additional money. So I got more efficient at work and got my assignments done on time but without overtime.

"I told you the kids handed me some weighty problems to solve. Well, I tackled the drug use first. At first Dino protested and said he could 'handle it.' But he didn't quit, and so through my company connections, I got him into a drug rehab program pronto. But it didn't work.

"I made phone calls on my lunch hour and got to know the programs of every applicable social-service agency. In this way, I found another procedure that included parents. What Dino and I learned at the all-day Saturday sessions, we discussed at supper with Irena and Marcos. No way did I want to repeat this experience with these kids, and I know they felt the same way. What Dino was going through really scared them. And that was good. He's been clean for two years now, and I partly owe that to the contract Dino and I have about drug use."

I asked details of the contract. "It's just a piece of paper I wrote up. It's a pledge between Dino and me. It says that if he stays clean one year, I help him buy wheels. If he stays clean two years, I give him some money so he can go to State—he wants to teach phys. ed. And if he stays clean through college, I'll help him get a place of his own. So I no longer have to pay for his drug use—he was stealing stuff from me and selling it to cover his drug costs—and the money I'm saving goes for things he wants. We both signed the contract, and we talk about it often. To be fair to the other kids, I'll see that they have ways to earn the things they want, too.

"You'd think that problem was the hardest, but the other problems took more of my time and attention. Even though his I.Q. is average, Marco thinks he isn't a good student, so he hates school. In junior high he started cutting classes and sometimes missing school for several days at a time. I got him into an extension school where the kids have special classes and certain jobs to do. After a year, he pleaded to go back to the regular high school.

"I made another of my famous contracts, a really simple one that said the first time he wasn't in school when he was supposed to be, it was back to the extension school. He's a social kid and likes his friends, so he makes sure he doesn't cut out of school even one class early. His teachers know of our contract and will notify me of any truancy. I actually think he's learning some things there, too. He has two study halls and a student mentor to help him get the work done.

"But Irena was the biggest problem. She had a mother who

thought that a slim body was all that really counted. Irena takes after me, sort of rounded. When she started school she began to get overweight. You should have heard Sylvia rail at her. To defend Irena I'd say she looked fine, but I knew she didn't.

"When there was no mother to watch her eating habits and encourage daily exercise, she ate even more. Then suddenly, she began to lose weight like magic. I thought it was an answer to my prayers until a school counselor called me in and told me my kid had bulimia.

"Wow, I soon found out more than I wanted to know about bingeing and purging. I found out why she suddenly left the table. I found out why our bathroom always smelled of room spray. I found out how she could eat a whole bag of cookies at a sitting. I felt helpless. I told Sylvia, but she had a new baby and said it was my problem. She was sure Irena would get over it. But she didn't. Feeling very helpless, I called to make an appointment with our family doctor, but a few days before we went, I was rescued by a friend.

"This woman from work saw us at a company picnic. She complimented me on my beautiful slim daughter. So I dumped the whole problem on this stranger—right there at the beach. It was then that Carleen admitted she'd had the same problem. We had other things in common, too. We were both divorced, we each had three teenagers, we worked in the same office, we liked baseball and camping.

"So, one thing led to another. We dated a bit, she got to know and really like Irena, and she told me how to get some help. They went clothes shopping together, they talked about over-eating, she even helped us *all* eat better—not the take-out pizza and frozen dinners we'd been living on.

"At that time Irena and I did most of the cooking, and Carleen sometimes came over with her kids and we all ate together.

Later that year we went camping together. Well, the eating disorder cure was moving right along and the relationship was moving right along too. The kids encouraged it. I even went shopping for a ring one Saturday, but I didn't buy one. Something wasn't right.

"Then it hit me. I wasn't really in love with Carleen. I *appreciated* her for all the help she was giving me. And it was nice having a friend for social occasions and companionship. In working out problems with these kids, I was pretty pressed emotionally and physically, and I thought it might be handy to have some help on a regular basis. But you don't marry someone because it's handy. At least I couldn't do that.

"Besides, I realized that Carleen was a package deal. And I didn't want to be 'The Brady Bunch' all over again. Somehow, three more teenagers didn't sound like much fun. It was then that Carleen got laid off at work, and that made me feel rotten. Now she was at our house even more. It was the whole gang night after night.

"One weekend I planned to tell her that I just wanted us to be friends. That sounds so stupid. I rehearsed my little talk over and over, but I never got to give it. That Friday afternoon she called to say that the company had recalled her, but for a job in Washington state. She had to move fast, as she was to start the following week. So we all went over to her house to help pack her van and the rented trailer. She kissed me lightly and said she hoped we'd keep in touch. We have, but I don't think anything more will ever come of it. Sure, I might remarry sometime, but not now.

"So this last year we've managed totally on our own—no big troubles, but lots of work. I've had to be more organized, more patient, more understanding than I thought I could ever be. Let me tell you some things that *have* worked here."

While Rob was talking, Irena came downstairs to start supper. She could hear us talking and occasionally she shouted a good idea from the kitchen. Dino and Marco sat down with us, too, and it was good to see that they acknowledged the family traditions and values that they had established together.

For example, they try to get together Sunday afternoon to plan the upcoming week. They settle who gets to use the car and who takes the school bus, who does the marketing and errands, how they will switch household tasks every month, and they plan at least one family event for each weekend.

Dino adds a few words about drugs. "Dad probably told you I had a problem. You know, I could be earning big money if I wanted to be dealing. It's really hard not to have a lot of money. But at least I make a little at my part-time job, I have my own car now, and soon I'll be going to college. Parties aren't easy—at friends' places there's a lot of temptations. If we get together *here*, the rules are no drugs, no booze, no smoking, no party crashers, and the music has to end by one in the morning."

Dino stops a moment and gets Rob's attention, then he continues: "Dad's always on hand, lurking about." Dino laughs, and adds, "No, he's really good about being out of sight most of the time. I went to a party last weekend, and would you believe, one of the parents at that house was also on hand to see we didn't get too wild. I guess when I have kids I'll be just as strict."

Marco is the shy one. I asked him how it was going in school. "I get mostly Cs. I've had some Ds and one B. Dad made a big deal over the B! I have no idea what I want to be or do after high school.

"Maybe I'll try to join the Marines or something like that. I probably will have to get better grades the next couple of years, and I don't know if I can do that. Everything takes me twice as long as anyone else to do. Maybe it's because I'm the middle guy in this family. It might be better to be the oldest and get privileges or be the youngest and get babied. But I'm gonna be cool and stay in school. Dad has made that clear to me. Right, Pops?" He looks at Rob affectionately.

At this point, Irena comes into the room, wiping her hands on an apron. "I don't want you to think I'm the only cook around here. These guys actually aren't too bad in the kitchen. We switch jobs every month, and so I've learned a lot of guy-stuff too. Last week Dino showed me how to change the oil filter on his car."

She went over and perched on Rob's knee teasingly stroking his face. Looking at me she said, "Now, will you *please* tell my dad I'm old enough to date. I can go to parties, but he won't let me go out on a real date until next year. So please tell him it's okay." And with that she returned to the kitchen.

Rob says that Irena has had to grow up a bit faster than normal, having to assume some of her mother's duties. And of all the children, she has missed Sylvia the most. "She goes over to see Sylvia and the baby, but that's not the same as having a mom in the house. There's a lot of things about growing-up girls that I'm clumsy or embarrassed about. I'm afraid Irena is learning most of what she needs to know from her friends. I'm glad that next year she'll have a health class at school."

He continues with his list of things that have worked for him. "You have to set some boundaries—what's acceptable, what isn't. And you have to enforce the rules with teens. I campus them or take the car keys when they don't follow the rules. No second chances, and they know that.

"We try to eat dinner together. It's a time for talk—not criticism. Often we go down to the beach and play volleyball. That's a good game for two generations. I'm not too swift, but I can usually keep up with them.

"I have to admit that I feel guilty about a few things. Maybe I didn't appreciate Sylvia enough, or maybe I didn't find out what was important in her life. If I marry again, I hope I'll do better. And, I wish I made more money—but who doesn't feel that way! Raising kids is expensive. But we're managing, and I can see we're making progress.

"Let me give one piece of advice for women who are getting divorced—women who are going to be the custodial parent. Stay on good terms with your ex. That way he'll help you chauffeur the kids to their endless activities, pay for special items and events, and spend time with the children. I guess that goes for men getting divorced, too. Why can't we all get along better?"

Challenges

Rob is doing well. He says he sees that light at the end of the tunnel. Still, there are areas that will require his attention:

1. Finding female role models for Irena
2. Keeping a watchful eye on Dino during his college years
3. Helping Marco find something he enjoys learning about
4. Making a life for himself now, so that he won't be lost when the last youngster leaves home

Some Solutions

1. *Finding female role models for Irena.*

These are important years as Irena moves from little girl to womanhood. Without relatives nearby, and with a disinterested ex-wife, Rob is relying on the school and Irena's friends to give her important information on growing up. Library books and a caring woman doctor could be good sources of authoritative information.

Certainly Carleen was a big help before she moved away, especially getting Irena over the bulimia and the causes behind it. But what Rob really needs is to find a woman who can be both a friend and an advisor to Irena. The Big Sister program is one good answer.

---

2. *Keeping a watchful eye on Dino during his college years.*

While Dino has his drug problem under control, the next few years are crucial in maintaining his ability to fight this addiction. Alcohol consumption is notoriously prevalent on college campuses. Researchers find that if a young adult can remain drug-free to age twenty-one, there is an excellent chance that he or she will never have to deal with that problem in later years.

College will bring new pressures and new friends. Rob will need to be just as interested in and attentive to Dino's life in college as he was during the high school years. Living at home means that Dino won't be in a dorm or his own apartment, and this is best under the circumstances. For want of something to do, leisure time is when drugs are most often used.

Rob should be alert to Dino's needing extra money or having extra money. These could be indications of using or dealing in drugs. Rob is aware that Dino's drug-using friends still call him and try to entice him back into his old ways. So far Dino has held to his new convictions.

3. *Helping Marco find something he enjoys learning about.*

Although Marco is being agreeable about attending high school, he's starting the next school year with below-average grades and no ideas for his life after graduation. He has two summers before graduation, and these could provide some work experiences for him—maybe enticing him to consider a trade school or helping him realize he needs better grades to go to college and learn a profession.

In past summers, Rob has kept Marco busy at camp or doing remedial school work. This summer would be a good time to encourage a summer job. This way Marco would have opportunities to see what it's like to hold down a job. Rob has a very tender spot in his heart for this young man, but it's important that his love be combined with a firm, steering hand.

Because Marco sometimes hangs out with Dino and his friends, it's amazing that he's kept clear of drugs. Now, when Dino is busy in college, will Marco feel adrift and turn to drugs? Rob hopes that Dino's bad experience will have enlightened Marco in this area. Extracurricular activities and sports could help him meet others his age and gain ideas for a productive future.

4. *Making a life for himself now, so that he won't be lost when the last youngster leaves home.*

Rob is working so hard at being father, mother, provider, counselor, and friend, that there's been little time for himself the past three years.

Carleen was a pleasant diversion as well as a friend who helped him through Irena's eating disorder. Now that she's no longer on the scene, he spends little or no time with friends of either sex. For his own well-being he needs to generate some regular and some impromptu occasions to be with his peers. The children are demonstrating responsibility in occasionally being on their own, and Rob should trust them to do the right things while he is having some enjoyment himself.

KEYS TO SUCCESS

In a culture that has long regarded youngsters as the mother's concern, Rob has shown that the qualities of love and nurturing are just as much in the man's domain. While many more men are *purposely* discovering the joys and perils of single fatherhood these days, Rob was plunged into the job with little training.

His success is based on his love for the children. The first thing he did was to get the family organized. He did this partly for his own sanity, but mainly because he didn't want them to miss out on any of the activities formerly in his wife's domain.

Next, he worked with them to set some rules. As he puts it, "I set the boundaries with love." These parameters helped his teenage trio understand their responsibilities concerning the home, driving, school, drugs, and caring for one another. He's learning to be more comfortable in discussing with them the challenges of dating and handling their own sexuality.

And when times got tough, he found he could call on others to help. School administrators and teachers, social agency workers, and a friend all stepped in to help overcome serious

CHAPTER NINE

Survival!

144 tested ideas to make single parenting more successful

IN MY SURVEYS, HUNDREDS OF single parents have shared their problems and frustrations, their hopes and successes with me. In doing so, many of them offered gems of advice that have worked for them. From these parents and others who are successfully enjoying family life, come these 144 best ideas.

Helping Yourself

You probably have three jobs: parent, homemaker, career person. At the same time, you want to have a life for yourself—and that takes talent! But keeping your eye on your goals and not being deterred by what others say or do, you'll succeed. As one single dad said, "Stay focused, it *does* get better!"

1 Take charge. For too long you've been at the beck and call of others, such as a spouse or parent. Now you are the chief person in your child's life. At last, you can do it your way. Write down your goals. Be sure they are realistic and attainable. Decide which goal is most important and begin to tackle it this week.

2 Take care of yourself. If you fall apart, the family could collapse. Schedule some "me time"—an hour at the gym, time in the jacuzzi, thirty minutes with a good book, a few moments just sitting and looking out a window. Because you love your children, it's important to fight for this time and be selfish about it. Many divorced wives say, "I used to do everything to please *him*; now I'm going to please myself and my children."

3 Get counseling if you need it. Find out how to feel contentment again. If your children see you happy, they will be happy too. Keep a positive attitude. Certainly divorce is serious; but it's not the end of the world and counseling can help. Find out if your company offers an employee-assistance program to help offset the cost.

4 Try forgiveness. This is tough, but bitterness and hatred don't advance your life, they hold it in the past. On paper, write something like this about your former spouse: "I forgive you for your apathy, argumentative attitude, drinking, womanizing, cruelty, abuse [write whatever you feel is true]." Sign your name. Next tear the page into little pieces and throw it away.

5 Keep your sense of humor. As one woman said, "Single parenting is easier than a difficult marriage. Now I have just two children; when married, I had three."

6 Cherish each day. You'll never get this one back. Accomplish something, no matter how small.

7 Say the words! Don't let the day end without telling your children how much you love them.

8 Don't be a yo-yo. Find things that calm you when emotions run high. When you feel a mood swing coming on, tell yourself how special and important you are to the family.

9 Make a list of the things you miss. Consider one subject each month and see how you can enjoy these pleasures once again. The "survey parents" listed these as the things most missed: regular companionship, extra income, help with discipline, someone who would get up during the night with a child, having another person in the house, someone to consult with on decisions, a way to get relief from the daily routine, a partner for social events, and another adult to talk with.

10 Keep a positive attitude. Children assess their own well-being by what is going on around them. If the custodial parent constantly feels depressed and hopeless, this erodes the child's sense of well-being and distorts realities to the point that the child has a skewed view of family life.

11 Criticism about parenting can't hurt you unless it is deserved. If you think you aren't the best caregiver, learn to be, or let the other spouse try. Women are *expected* to be good caregivers; so when they make mistakes, they get criticized. Men who have custody get by with much more since there is little expectation of their parenting abilities. Do what you think is best, not what you're pressured into doing.

12 Give yourself time. Grow from experiences, learn from them. Move onward. Move from the known to the unknown, from the familiar to the unfamiliar like a swan floating on a lake. The transition from marriage to being single doesn't have to take its toll on you.

Dealing with an ex-spouse

Most husbands and wives spend time thinking about how much they resent their ex's, but it's a waste of time neither parent can afford. There must be and will be times you'll need to communicate with each other, so it's much easier if you're at least civil. And when you think of your ex, try to recall something pleasant.

13 When something bugs you, don't let it take over your mind and your conversation with others. Rather than bore or distress your friends, create a written "gripe list." When you look at it later, I bet some of the things won't seem so important. Cross those off the list! List hurtful things so you don't have to spend time thinking about them. And once the list is written, you can put it away and never look at it again. But if you put the list where you'll see it, keep crossing off things until you no longer need a list.

14 Don't be rushed when an ex-spouse asks you to do something. Take your time to think through the issue. Communicate only when you're well rested and calm. Write down the decisions you've agreed upon. Put a date on them. Repeat them to the other spouse at the end of the discussion so there's no misunderstanding.

15 Write down dates for meetings, visitations, and so forth, and always be prompt. Never play games by not turning up when you're expected.

16 When you first separate, agree that the divorce is to be between the two parents and that the kids are not going to be brought in as pawns. Together, tell the children that you two will always be their parents and that you will always love them.

17 Decide well in advance the arrangements for vacations and major holidays. Sometimes sharing holidays together works well if you and your ex-spouse are friendly.

18 When a child marries, put aside the past. As a new family starting out, the bride and groom need your unconditional love. This is no time to be bitter or try to get even by withholding invitations or by making a scene at the ceremony or reception.

19 When telephoning an ex, always begin the conversation with, "Is this a good time for you to talk?"

20 Remind yourself that there was a time when you loved your ex-spouse. Remember the good times.

Talking with kids about divorce

Silence doesn't make it go away. Before youngsters hear rumors, tell them that there is going to be a divorce. In simple terms, let them know what it's going to be like before, during, and after.

21 Regularly reassure children that you love them very much and you can work things out as a family. Remember to express your love every single day.

22 Kids are smart. They know what is going on, so don't try to hide things from them. Don't ask their advice about the divorce, but tell them enough to satisfy them.

23 Don't "bad mouth" your ex-spouse. Make a list of good qualities and positive experiences that you've shared. Mention these rather than getting down into the dirt. When you put down your spouse, you put down your child's heritage.

24 Don't build up the spouse unrealistically. You don't want kids to think, "If Dad [or Mom] was so great, why didn't you two stay married?" When it fits into the conversation, it's okay to calmly mention shortcomings without being overly critical.

25 Talk through the pain and anger that a child may feel. One daughter couldn't understand why her father opted not to spend time with her. Understanding the circumstances helped to lift the low self-esteem caused by the apparent abandonment.

26 Offer youngsters a framed picture of your ex-spouse, or a picture of the entire family.

27 Use in-the-car time to good advantage. Talk about anything that interests a child—school, fun, food, the divorce, fears, excursions, holidays.

28 Reassure children that they were not the cause of the divorce. You may have to do this many times.

When a spouse has died

Children need to understand. They need to grieve. Grief and anger and bewilderment are not the private domains of the remaining spouse. Helping a child to endure the loss also helps the surviving parent through the tragedy.

29 Be sure young children understand that the deceased parent is not going to suddenly return. Explain death in the framework of your own beliefs.

30 Sometimes, in anger, a child has "wished" a parent dead. Now that parent has died, and a great sense of guilt can set in. With forgiving tender love, explain to the child that we all feel very angry at times and that she is not responsible for the death.

31 Don't let a child take the place of the missing parent by forcing him or her into adult situations. Let a child remain a child in duties around the house, in decision-making, in activities.

32 Keep family pictures on hand and talk about the good times. Offer a youngster a picture of the deceased parent.

33 When facing a challenge, consider together what the deceased spouse might suggest.

34 Don't make the absent parent into a saint. Share successes and failures, talking with sincerity and good humor.

35 Although youngsters may remind you of the deceased spouse, don't emphasize how much alike they are. If a child thinks he's "just like Dad," he may fear that he, too, will die.

36 Consider a small memorial to the absent parent. One of the nicest is to plant a tree in his or her honor.

37 Use true examples of how much the deceased parent loved each child.

When youngsters visit the other parent

It can be threatening to you to let your children visit the other parent and perhaps that parent's new spouse and family. Don't let your anxiety rub off. Look at it this way: you're going to get some free time for yourself!

38 Have the youngsters ready on time with suitable clothing, books, and toys, plus a little spending money. As they leave tell them to have a truly great time!

39 Suggest something about you that they can share with the other parent about you: your work, a book you're reading, a place you and the kids visited, a class you're taking. Tell them it's okay to talk about you in these casual ways.

40 When children return, don't quiz them about the other spouse, but have a normal interest in what they did. If you don't see the ex-spouse when the children come home, a telephone call can express their thanks and yours.

41 If children tell how nice it was at Dad's place (or Mom's), express your pleasure that they had a good time. Don't indulge in comparisons!

42 If children report things they were permitted to do on the visit, but that they are not permitted to do at home, simply say, "That's the way it works there, but this is the way it is here." Don't judge.

43 Don't become alarmed if a child threatens to go live with the other parent. If it is legally proper, you may want to let this happen for a trial period. Statistics show that about 90 percent of these youngsters eventually return to the first custodial parent.

44 One difference between the custodial parent's home and the ex-spouse's home is the change in routine. The noncustodial parent may be more permissive, not having to deal with the child on a continuing basis. The custodial parent should give youngsters as many choices and opportunities as possible without spoiling them.

45 If the other parent doesn't take a deep interest in the children, just be glad that you do. Don't say, "Dad [or Mom] doesn't care enough about you to be concerned with what you're doing."

46 Keep good relations with your ex-spouse, so that you can rearrange the set visiting times when you have conflicting plans or when there is something special you want to do on your own.

When you have custody

About fifteen million children under age eighteen are living with a single parent. Ninety percent of the children live with a single mother. Either way, raising children is a privilege, not a punishment. Make the most of it each day.

47 Don't confuse homemaking with parenting. Your children are far more important than vacuuming.

48 Find time to talk. Research shows that kids and parents have only about three minutes of meaningful conversation a day. Go for much, much more.

49 Don't encourage a child's fantasies about her parents getting together again. Even if you consider this a possibility, keep it to yourself at the present.

50 Strive to find adult friends for your child. Single mothers should find male role models; fathers should find female ones. It's important for a child to be comfortable with both sexes.

51 Use mealtimes to coordinate upcoming family activities and talk about that day's events. Conversation thrives when you eat at a table with the television set turned off.

52 Loneliness hurts both adults and kids. Sometimes a hands-on pet (a dog as opposed to a fish) provides companionship for a responsible youngster.

53 Children need reassurance that you care. Put a short love note, a cartoon, or a picture in a child's lunch box. Don't be so busy with routine parenting that you forget to express your love. Say the words "I love you." Show your love in hugs, kisses, and good deeds.

54 Children with single parents are left alone much more than children in two-parent families. See that your child knows safe procedures for locking the house, answering the phone, using the 911 emergency number, knowing where you can be reached, using a key, and so forth.

55 Mothers Day and Fathers Day can be hard. Be considerate of feelings. Help your children choose a card and small gift for the absent parent. Perhaps that parent will do the same for you on your day.

56 Set parameters for your children. Be firm; be consistent. Next to love, what they most need is discipline.

57 Some one-parent families are so rushed in the morning that they don't eat breakfast. This shortchanges a child who is whisked off to school hardly awake and poorly fed. Make the needed time for this meal and the time for love and reassuring conversation before parting for the day.

58 If you won't be home when your child returns home, plan to call the child or have the child call you. Give some direction to the hours before you return home (play, homework, chores, supper preparation). A short, upbeat conversation is all it takes. If you can't call home, leave a list or a cassette tape.

59 Don't deprive your child of learning to be responsible. Each day give at least thirty minutes of "work" to a child (making a salad, feeding the dog, dusting the living room, doing the dishes, watering the lawn).

60 Try to spend the hour after dinner with your child. Let this be a time for talks, walks, games, crafts, reading—any form of togetherness. Then take time to tuck in younger children and chat with older ones before bed. This lets you reassure children that you love and care for them.

61 Divide the weekend into segments for errands, home maintenance, kids' tasks, sporting events, social events for kids, social events for you. Do things together: shop, hike, go to church. Plan at least one special event for each weekend—it doesn't have to be costly.

62 Keep watch on your child's emotional well-being. One dad tells how he and his son get rid of their anger. They take two pillows and beat them on the bed with all their might. With each whack, they tell something that bugs them. By the time they're finished, they both feel better.

63 When the other parent doesn't take advantage of visitation rights, a child may ask, "Doesn't Daddy [or Mommy] like me?" Explain that the parent *does* truly care, but that raising a child is such a big job, the other parent wasn't ready for it and so he (or she) went away.

64 Be generous to the noncustodial parent. Remember the Golden Rule: Do unto others as you would have them do unto you. Setting a civilized example can bring you blessings.

When you don't have custody

Studies show that noncustodial parents don't see their children on a regular basis—even though they have the right to do so. Almost half had *no* contact over a five-year period!

65 Don't give up. Don't be discouraged. Many noncustodial parents lose interest after a while—especially if the ex-spouse makes contacting the child difficult. Remember, your input is important to your child.

66 Take a special interest in your child's schooling. Offer to visit the school, attend parent/teacher meetings, and school events when the child participates.

67 Mark in your date book each year the special times to be in touch. These include birthdays, Valentine's Day, Easter, the last day of school, graduation, Halloween, Thanksgiving, Christmas, or those events that are meaningful to you and your child. Don't let a child think you've forgotten.

68 Use a variety of forms of communication: letters and greeting cards, postcards when you travel, a note or call after a visitation, regular telephone calls, photos of things you've done together with a note attached. Modern methods of communication can help. One dad sends a FAX now and then—

that makes the child feel important! Consider recording a cassette about your activities, or a video of you and your work and home.

69 Bedtime stories can still be your domain. Get books from the library and read them onto cassette tapes. Do enough stories so that a child can hear you read a story each night for an entire week.

70 Make your visiting child feel a part of the family, not a guest. Don't try to impress the child with fancy food or gifts. Once you overindulge him, it's hard to stop. At the custodial house, there are many things that absolutely must be done. So let a child visiting you have some choices as to what to do. But include some work projects in these choices to keep a healthy balance.

71 Often one parent has more money than the other. Cultural entertainment is often the first to be cut out when money is short. If you're the more affluent, consider giving your child some special experiences (as opposed to "things"): short trips, excursions to a musical or symphony. Don't flaunt your affluence. One child said, "At first I liked the way Dad spent money when I visited, but now I hate him for making Mom and me live with so little."

72 Family roots shouldn't be lost because of a divorce. Take time to share with your child your family's background, neighborhood, foods, traditions. When possible, visit the grandparents and other relatives. It gives a child the feeling of belonging to two families, and this can be twice as beneficial as just one.

73 Know your child sufficiently well that you don't have to resort to money gifts. Prior to gift-giving occasions, ask for a "wish list." Shop where things are exchangeable in case you guess wrong. Don't choose gifts that will break and be tossed out. Consider giving a subscription to a children's magazine, a piece of sports equipment, a small rocking chair—things that can often remind the child of you.

74 Rather than shopping for food in advance of the visit, go to the market *with* the youngster and let her choose the foods you'll make and eat together. Encourage new food choices.

75 Surprise your ex-spouse. During the child's visit, make a batch of cookies together. Eat some, let the child take some home to the other parent.

76 Take some pressure off the custodial parent. Take your child clothes shopping. Or offer to attend his recital. The spouse with custody will appreciate this, and *you* may find that even recitals can be fun!

77 Become an expert for your child and teach him or her one of your skills: woodworking, sewing, fishing, tap dancing, gardening, computer, tennis.

78 Go to the library together and borrow some books. Read these together before bed. Learn the kinds of books your child likes and have some on hand for the next visit.

79 Keep a list of projects that you'll pay kids to do. That way they can earn a little spending money. Cleaning the garage, putting up the screens, painting a fence—something you might pay someone else to do.

80 Don't spoil the children—this really bugs the custodial parent. Ask what means of discipline the custodial parent uses (time-out, deprivation) and follow it.

81 Take an interest and educate yourself in the big problems youngsters face today. Look for newspaper clippings that will make an easy opening to the discussion. Talk about sex, gangs, drugs, alcohol, smoking, speeding, suicide. Be a listening ear. Encourage good values.

82 Provide a drawer or shelf where the child can keep her own things and leave them between visits.

83 Have on hand some amusements suitable to the child's age. For younger children: building blocks, puppets, a small bike, little racing cars. For older children: a doorway gym bar, construction toys, sports equipment, trivia, and board games.

84 Sleeping out under the stars can be a great bonding experience. A cookout, some games, and talking in the dark make for a memorable event.

85 When a child goes home, slip into the suitcase a little message of love.

Support systems

Face it. You can't do it all alone. Even two-parent families require the help of others. Don't be so proud you miss out on these helpful connections.

86 Talk with your child about the people—kids and adults—she enjoys. Arrange time for her to be with them. These opportunities let others express their care, which not only helps you, it helps them, too.

87 Seek support in these categories: nearby relatives, neighbors, friends from your work place, school teachers and counselors, athletic coaches, club leaders, religious advisors, social services, and groups such as Big Brothers or Big Sisters.

88 Don't divorce your in-laws. Unless there is a very good reason to cut them off, let them see and enjoy their grandchildren.

89 While your child is well, look ahead as to what you'll do if he is sick and must miss school. Care for sick children can be very expensive. Find a nearby caregiver at a price you can afford. Prior to a time you need help, invite the person over to get acquainted with your home and family.

90 Find another single parent and work out trades that give each of you free time while the other watches both families.

91 Carefully choose your daycare or after-school facility. Consider personal care and attention, sanitary standards, nutrition, curriculum, child/adult ratio, your privilege of dropping in unexpectedly, and so forth.

92 Don't over-program your child with clubs and activities, thinking you are "making up" for his not having two parents. Two group activities a week is plenty.

93 Be a smart single parent. Subscribe to a magazine for single parents. Join a single parents' club. (See chapter 12 for ideas.)

94 Enrich your child's life by your own interest and self-education in subjects you can share: computers, music, art, literature, politics, world history, economics, the environment.

Money matters/Income stretching

How do you manage on a fifteen-thousand-dollar income when your spouse is earning sixty thousand? It isn't easy! Not having enough money is the chief complaint of the single custodial parent. Learn how to be a happy tightwad. There's even a newsletter on this subject—details in chapter 12.

95 It's absolutely necessary to have a budget. This is the only way you'll know where your money goes and where you are spending too much. You may not be able to adhere strictly to it at first, but keep trying.

96 With teenagers, share the budgeting. Let them suggest where cuts can be made. Be sure to give them opportunities to earn some of their own discretionary funds.

97 Let children over ten have a clothing budget. Suggest good buys, but let them choose for themselves. It can be a real learning experience to decide between one expensive shirt and two bargain ones.

98 Have a neighborhood toy exchange. Children bring in toys that no longer interest them. For each toy, they get a ticket that entitles them to choose a new toy. This is no-cost fun and saves a lot of money.

99 Since it is much cheaper to cook at home than eating out or buying prepared foods, make simple menus of home-cooked foods. This is a good TV-time job. If you take turns having a young assistant cook or letting a teen take charge with *you* as assistant, meal preparation can be a nice togetherness time.

100 Plan to put aside something for savings on a regular basis. Even if it can only be a very small amount, *start* to save. Remember, child support usually ends with high school graduation. And way down the road, you'll want extra funds at retirement.

101 Attend garage sales and go to thrift shops with your children. See who can find the most useful bargain.

102 The teenage years are the most expensive. See that your child knows how to sew fashionable clothing. Borrow fancy dress-up clothes for proms. Together with your teen, decide what you can do without, or pare down other expenditures to help cover teen expenses.

103 Vacations are a luxury most families can't afford. Read travel magazines and keep a file of bargain trips. Here's where you can call for help from out-of-town friends who may have a spare room. Consider out-of-door vacations at parks and beaches—camping out is inexpensive fun.

Managing alone

So you were accustomed to leaning on someone else for changing the light bulbs and pruning the hedge? Most single parents say that managing the family alone was the biggest adjustment. But they learned to cope! Many said that they liked *not* having to consult or compromise on many matters.

104 Get smart. Learn to do things on your own. Let your kids be in charge of some things (like the taping of shows on the VCR).

105 Take a night class in home management or simple car maintenance.

106 Don't invite someone over just to do household tasks for you. You'll feel better if you "pay" with dinner or a movie. When someone offers to look at the leaky faucet, accept. Then watch, ask questions, and learn how to do it yourself next time.

107 Start a good filing system that includes divorce papers, budget, warranties/guarantees, insurance, letters to write, a file for each youngster for health and school records, clippings about things to do together, and a wish list of things you want to buy when there is money.

108 Get organized. Work at a desk. Do some housecleaning project every other week. Start a load of wash each time you pass the machine. Do repairs once a week. Do two things at once, such as cooking dinner and testing a child's spelling.

109 One of the best sources of comfort when managing a family alone is a belief in a supreme being. Knowing God means you're never alone.

110 Rearrange the furniture, lamps, bric-a-brac, and pictures at your house. This is a lot cheaper than buying new items or being dissatisfied with the same stuff in the same places.

111 Have a bulletin board in the kitchen or family room. Use it for messages, good schoolwork, and the family calendar.

112 Collect souvenirs from school events, ball games, and excursions, as well as postcards, report cards, and extra-special school work. Put these things in a drawer and at the end of each year, put them in a scrapbook. You'll enjoy seeing all the highlights in your life.

113 Be creative in finding time to be with your child. One mother has made an arrangement at work to skip two lunches a week in return for leaving two hours early one day. She picks up her children after school each Wednesday and they go on a short excursion together.

Social life

You know what they say about all work and no play. It's important to your well-being to have social times. That doesn't mean hunting for a new spouse; it means enjoying life right now, as you are.

114 Don't continually turn down offers from friends to do things together. They may take you seriously and leave you alone.

115 Contrary to the popular notion that bars are good meeting places, most single parents cite these three better places to look for new friends: a class, a church event, an introduction by a mutual acquaintance.

116 Plan some social times on a regular basis: weekly bowling, dinner out with office friends, a movie with the kids, church.

117 Others are lonely too! Invite your apartment-house mates or those who live on your block for a potluck get-together.

118 See that your children have a good social life. Help them plan something to do with friends each weekend. Since you probably are at work during the week, the weekend time can be used to have youngsters at your house. Let the parents who watch over kids during the weekdays know you appreciate their interest.

119 Even though you are very busy as a single parent, volunteer as a leader or chaperon for some youth activities. Besides showing your child that you're interested in his social life, it is also an opportunity to make friends with other adults.

120 When out socially, don't discuss the messy divorce. Even if they don't object, people really don't want to hear about it. Save your soul-searching and complaints for your best friend, your close relatives, or your pillow.

121 Reading makes you a more interesting person. Read every day. Find the time on the bus, while eating lunch, waiting in the dentist's office, while taking a bath, just before falling asleep.

122 Don't let home life revolve around television. Play games, go for a bike ride, read books together, bake cookies, write a letter, telephone friends. Invite friends over for an evening of games.

123 Don't stop taking photos just because there's only one parent in the picture. Pictures are an excellent way of reliving good memories of past events with friends and family. And you'll be encouraged to plan some good times for the present.

124 Start new traditions such as Saturday breakfast in bed or evening walks or putting a nickel in a jar for using a swear word. Invite another family and have a popcorn-and-apple supper on a Sunday night.

Dating

Once burned or hurt, many single parents hesitate to ever date again, while others jump into new relationships in hopes of finding the right person immediately. The questions, "Am I worthy of a new relationship?" and "Can I trust again?" and "What will the kids think?" are ones that need to be settled first.

125 Before you start to date again, explain to youngsters that your dating is similar to their having friends. You are interested in companions of your own age, not necessarily someone to marry.

126 Start slowly. After a few dates with the same person, include the kids. Don't start with a meal at home; choose neutral territory instead. A good first time together is going for ice cream or a movie.

127 Set standards of child behavior for when a date will be at your house. Tell youngsters that you expect good manners, good conversation, no arguments, and no personal questions.

128 The first dinner at home should be a casual one—possibly even a cookout with foods kids like. Save the candlelight supper for later.

129 Tell children that you are not trying to replace their father (or mother). Although they may eventually get a stepfather, their father will always be their father.

130 Tell children that you are not dating because you're dissatisfied with their company. Explain that they will eventually leave home, and at that time you will need a full life of your own.

131 Sometimes dates are spontaneous. This isn't easy for the single parent with young children. Find a sitter or relative that you can call on short notice.

132 Don't force kids to give advice on which date they like best. After a date or a time together when they were included, find out what they did or didn't enjoy. Let the emphasis be on the activity, not the person.

133 The matter of you and your date sleeping together is a very delicate one. It's better to avoid this—better for the children and better for you. Most single parents in my survey advised against having a date stay overnight. If you must indulge, don't be sneaky. Be up-front with teens since you're probably discouraging premarital sex for them. Once you set a double standard, you're in trouble. Celibacy *is* a viable alternative.

134 Before or after a date, spend time with the children so that they don't feel the date is taking you away from them. After all, the kids have had you all to themselves, and it is natural for them to resent this intrusion.

135 If you don't really care about furthering a relationship, don't let your children become attached to that person.

136 Until you're ready for a major commitment, date several different people. Don't be rushed into a new relationship.

Remarriage

What's your reason for marrying again? Financial security? To be a two-parent family? Loneliness? To show others that you're desirable? How about love, common interests, and trust—a remarriage built on those has the best chance of success.

137 Since it was probably a painful experience to end the first marriage, think a lot about the ramifications of marrying again. Since teenage problems and discipline can be divisive, one mother decided not to remarry until the youngsters were out of high school. That way her new relationship would get a good start.

138 Don't marry to give the children a father (or mother). You want to love the person enough to live together long after the kids are gone.

139 Before marriage, talk about finances, discipline, how you'll settle differences. Discipline of children is the biggest challenge of second marriages, and the biggest reason for second divorces!

140 Carefully note the reaction of the proposed new spouse to situations with your children—especially situations that are upsetting. If he or she can't manage now, before marriage, it will probably be worse when you're under one roof.

141 When you think you have found the right new spouse, gradually introduce him or her to the family. Listen to comments, but make up your own mind.

142 With the children's input, talk about how the new spouse will interact with the family, and what will be his or her "place." Is this person going to be a new dad (or mom) or mom's new husband? Whatever the decision, respect for the new spouse is all-important.

143 Include youngsters in the wedding so that they feel part of the new marriage. Don't include them on the honeymoon, though.

144 Consider the possibility of the children being adopted by the new spouse. This might be a legal possibility and is often helpful for very young children. Many older kids feel comforted by it, but some definitely don't.

❖ ❖ ❖

Remember, learning to be a partnership with your first spouse took time and patience. Give yourself the same learning time to be a good single parent. Only then should you consider a new partnership.

CHAPTER TEN

Tattle-tales

What kids say about life with a single parent

TUNE IN TO THE YOUNG GEN-eration and hear both the good and the bad about growing up in a house with just one parent. From inter-views and my survey, I've found some extremely hon-est comments! You can learn a lot from—and even smile a bit at—these wise and witty but heart-felt remarks.

DIVORCE DIALOGUE

"Who did they think they were kidding—all smiley in front of us and then keeping us awake half the night with their arguments?"

"My dad made it very clear that I hadn't done anything wrong. For sure *I* didn't cause the divorce. They still love me, but he and Mom just weren't happy together."

155

"I'm glad they stayed together until I started high school. I know it was hard for them, but at least I was old enough to understand and love both of them."

"Sticking together for the sake of the kids is junk. I was so happy when they got divorced. No more bicker, bicker. No more making me the middle man."

"I've had better times with my dad since he and Mom split. He pays some attention to us now."

"My dad has custody now. It's almost as if my mom doesn't exist. She couldn't wait to go away with her boyfriend. They said they had me to help their marriage, but I don't think I helped."

"I was pretty mad at first. But now I've gotten used to it. Actually I ended up with two moms and two dads. I've nick-named my mom's new husband 'Pops Two' and my dad's wife is 'Mom Two.'"

"Don't believe that kids can be kept out of it. I hurt, I cried, I ran away. When my parents divorced, they divorced me, too."

"What happened between them is over. I still love my parents and they love me. That's what counts."

VISITATION TALES

"The judge set it up all orderly like. What a joke! My folks play mind-games with each other by messing up the visitation."

"It's great. I have a room and places to keep my stuff at my dad's condo. He never misses his turn. We don't do much that's special; we just act like a family."

"Dad tries to buy me. He takes me to the toy store at the mall, out for dinner, out for a movie. I'd rather stay at his place and talk or look at TV."

"She's never on time. I get so tired sitting on my suitcase on the curb, waiting for her to come and pick me up."

"It's creepy. We don't even talk about Mom."

"All we talk about is Mom. Dad really quizzes me about what she's doing and who she's dating. I think I'll make up some stories."

"At first, my mom had me for weekends and summer vacations. But each year, there's less and less time together. I'm afraid of losing her."

"The divorce screwed me up. Now they're doing it to me again with custody battles. I'm afraid of what they'll think of next."

"Mom says I come home and talk sassy and won't do my chores. She says it's Dad's bad influence. Sure, it's fun at Dad's and no fun here with Mom. That's not my fault."

"My dad has two other kids now. When I go to visit, he sits all three of us down and tells us what we must do and what we can do, how we should be respectful, and what there is to do that's fun."

"We never saw our dad as much as we do now. He doesn't have any distractions so he focuses in on the two of us for a whole weekend."

"Here's my rules for kids. 1. Be ready to go. Have clothes, toothbrush, a book, and catcher's mitt in the bag. 2. Clean up after yourself at Dad's place even though he's sloppy. 3. Don't knock the food. 4. Try to like his girlfriends. 5. Ask him what he'd like to do, or stay home. 6. Take the sheets off the bed when you leave. 7. Call him up when you get home. 8. Don't tell Mom stuff she doesn't need to hear."

"When I go to visit Dad, right away I tell him something nice about Mom. When I get home, right away I tell Mom something nice about Dad. That way they don't grill me."

MONEY MATTERS

"I'm never going to get divorced. Divorced people are poor."

"I was about seven years old when Mom got divorced. She sat me down and explained our money problems now that Dad had left. She had a chart of what we could afford to buy and what we had to save. We talked about what I could do to help. It wasn't as bad as I thought it would be."

"I got a job when I was thirteen so I could help."

"Dad's place is a lot nicer than Mom's and mine. I like to go there. He buys me toys and new clothes. I keep these at his house."

"When I was in high school, I found out how much child support Dad was paying. I was really shocked because Mom always talked poor. We ate okay, but I never got any new clothes or sports equipment—but Mom always had new stuff."

"Money doesn't help the hurt to go away."

"My parents try to buy us. My brothers and I don't like that. At first it was fun 'cause of all the things we got. Now it's kind of a game of who can do the most for us. I wish they'd get married to each other again."

"Sure, my dad earns more than my mom. But my mom cares more about me."

"What a shock when they split up! My world ended at age

sixteen. There was no money to live the 'good life' we used to have together."

"Yes, we have less money. It makes me mad. I'm going to marry a rich man and when I get divorced, I'll keep all his money."

"They got divorced over money arguments. Now all I hear is Mom calling Dad about when the check is coming. She's going to get a hook on his paycheck so we get our share. He was able to come up with money before, so what's changed?"

"I'm only in second grade but my friends tell me that when your folks get divorced, the judge gets to keep everyone's money."

"I suppose we're living on less money. I know we live in a less good neighborhood, and I know I get fewer presents and less spending money. But I'm living with a parent who really loves me and wants me. That's a lot more than many people in this world have."

Yes, There Are Some Advantages!

"It's great. The folks used to spend time with each other. Now they just have me—Mom on weekdays, Dad on weekends. I love being the center of attention."

"They don't argue anymore. They just look sad at each other when I get picked up or dropped off."

"Stepmothers aren't as bad as the storybooks tell."

"We feel important, my sister and me. Dad and Mom think a lot more about what we want and how we feel."

"At home I have to share a bedroom with my baby sister. At Dad's I have a room all to myself and there are zoo animals on the wallpaper."

"When my folks were married, Daddy never wanted to help with my homework. Now he has to when I'm at his place and I found out that he's really good at it. He's explained some hard math stuff and helped me get better grades."

"Mom never goes out without me. That's good."

"I get two Christmas mornings and two birthday parties."

"Before, I was an only child. When Mom remarried I got two big brothers. They're more good than bad."

"I get telephone calls from Dad and Grandma and Grandpa. They want to know how I'm doing."

"When I get married after high school, I'll have a big wedding because I have lots more relatives now. My folks each remarried into big families. We have so much more fun since the divorce."

GRUMBLES AND GRIPES

"Why can't they let it rest! Each one says such rotten stuff about the other. I can't believe any of it's true."

"They think I'm some kind of spy. When I'm with one, that one asks such weird personal questions about the other. Wish I could ask them to talk direct to the other."

"The marriage was their mistake. The divorce was their solution. The person most hurt was me."

"I don't know if I want to get married. Mom says all men are slime, and I'm beginning to believe it."

"They said they loved each other. I don't know if I want to love someone so much that when they're gone I just cry and cry."

"My mom died. My dad won't talk about it. There are things I'd like to know."

"How can I earn an extra hundred bucks a week so I don't have to listen to Mom pleading for money?"

"They got divorced fifteen years ago and Mom's still angry."

"I know my parents feel responsible for my problems. Maybe they should feel a little guilt. I do."

"Isn't there life ahead? Can't we forget the past?"

MY PARENT IS GOING ON A DATE!

"Let's be up-front. Quit this line about going to the mall. I know that my mom is really meeting someone and going out on a date."

"It's wonderful. My mom looks so pretty now. She smiles. She dresses nicely. I don't care if she marries this guy. At least he's brought her out of the pits."

"Whenever a guy is coming over, she gives us this lecture on being good, polite, and quiet. We try, but it's hopeless. Let's face it, who would want to date or marry a woman with five kids? We never see any of the guys more than once."

"When a date is coming for dinner, do we ever eat good!"

"It's so funny when my mom's date comes to pick her up. Our sitter asks, 'And what time will you be home?'"

"Beware when your dad says that he has someone special he wants you to meet. It's probably his next wife."

"My parents both date. They always ask if I like the person they're dating. These people are okay by me. But the real question is, do *they* like the person. After all, they have to live with them. And maybe they will have to divorce them. I don't want to be in the middle or be responsible, so I don't give any advice."

"I love my dad's current girlfriend, but I love my mom, too. I hope she understands that."

"My dad died when I was a baby so this new guy seems like an all right person to be my new dad."

"Don't expect me to call her [the father's new wife] Mom. She will never, never, never replace my mom."

"My dad tells me not to sneak around. I'm seventeen, and I know what I'm doing when I date. But he sure sneaks around, and he's so immature for his age."

"I'm afraid that my mom will marry just to be married."

AND THEN THERE IS SEX . . .

"I'm tired of being told to go to my room and go to bed. I know what my dad's up to."

"My biggest concern is that both my folks are dating new people and really don't seem to have much information about abstinence and safe sex. I wonder if I should have a talk with them."

"It's nice for him to put his arms around my mom, but I think it's too soon for her to have a serious relationship."

"Mom asked me what I thought about Ken staying overnight. I said it was fine for him to have my room and I'd sleep in with her. I don't think that's what she had in mind."

"What's all this talk she gives us about moderation and purity. If my mom's supposed to be my role model, is she practicing what she's preaching?"

"I love for my mom to have companionship. But can't it move ahead a little more slowly?"

"I'm going to have this guy as my live-in stepdad for the next hundred years. I'd like to tell my mom how I feel, but she doesn't ask."

"Dad says it's different for him since men need more sex. That isn't what he told me when I was twelve."

"Mom says it's different because she's been married before. I face the same problems on high school dates, and I don't see what difference that makes."

"We're all going to this mountain retreat for a weekend. I think it's supposed to be like a trial marriage. Is this the way my parents did it?"

"I've told some big lies, but none as big as I'm hearing, now that each of my parents has joined the dating game. They must think I'm really naive or totally stupid."

LOVE IS THE LIBERATOR

"Happiness for my mother is what's important. My dad put her through hell and I hope she finds someone to love who really loves her."

"So we don't have much money or any extras. We have love again in our house."

"Dad says that money makes the world go 'round. Mom says that love makes the world go 'round. I side with my mother."

"I used to think that things we could buy were most important to me. I either grew older or smarter because I now know that caring is what counts."

"A lot of my friends are into the material scene, you know. Most of the music we listen to emphasizes that. I'm so glad that my parents, now divorced, gave me the greatest gift in the world: their love."

"Although my dad died when I was in grade school, the love he shared with me will last my whole lifetime."

"So there was a divorce, and a nasty one at that. But after three years, we're emotionally healed and ready to love again."

"Love—no one can take that away from me."

"It's a two way street: to love and to be loved. I live on that street."

CHAPTER ELEVEN

Looking Back and Looking Ahead

A plan for better single parenting

WHAT DO YOU DO NOW THAT you've read this book? Reading a book can be just an escape from reality *unless* it rewards you with an intriguing plot or useful ideas. I hope this book has done both of these things for you.

Certainly the "plots," the true stories of how other single parents are succeeding, can supply you with inspiration to go forward. And their useful ideas can spur you onward, too. Now it's up to you to put it all together for your own precious family.

GIFTS FOR YOU

There are things to learn from the story of each single parent in this book. Actually these brave people are providing you with priceless gifts.

165

Think back to Lauren, the chemist who left New England for the West. She gives you the gift of learning how to trust again. This came as she put aside the anger and realized that the problem wasn't hers, but her ex-husband's. She found that you don't have to carry someone else's burden. Lauren recognizes that she has to raise her daughter alone, but she's giving it her best shot and she's trusting others to help along the way.

Few of us can forget Nora, who saw so much grief as two men she loved died. Her gift to you is one of great faith in God. Maybe that's an answer for you, too. She says she could not have survived without that faith. Now with her sons, she is tackling their educational challenges and her own loneliness, knowing that she is never truly alone.

Troy is breaking new ground for both fathers and mothers. He teaches us that we can all *learn* to be good parents. His gift is encouraging you to educate yourself boldly, refusing to be put down by traditional roles for men or women. It's inevitable that some single parents are going to break new ground in liberating all parents from bias. You can join Troy in being one of those parents.

For Linda, whose biological clock was ticking, it was a matter of facing up to a problem and looking for solutions. That's a gift we'd all like—the ability to take a challenge and win. Now that she's solved the question of single motherhood, she's tackling the frustrations that go with it.

It took more than twenty years for Josie to fight her way from welfare mother to a college graduate. Her gift to you? Never give up! She had the fierce determination to hold her family together, and now she can do even more by directing that determination to help others survive.

Denice gives the gift of hope—hope for a better tomorrow without the abuse of the past. To bring Denice's hope from promise to fulfillment, she is giving her daughter the greatest gifts—self-confidence and unconditional love.

And Rob has helped us all to understand the teenage years. His gift is the bold reminder to "Get help" when there's a problem. And along with getting help, it is necessary for Rob to "Get a life." Single parents must look ahead to the time when there are no youngsters under the roof and their time will be more their own.

These courageous parents and hundreds of others who contributed to this book can *point* the way for you, but they can't *do* the work for you. Even though you may have wonderful support from friends, relatives, and organizations, sooner or later you have to jump in with both feet and go about succeeding on your own. It's up to *you* to do it.

Go Do It!

When does this "doing it" begin? It can begin today. You've read about what other families have done, and now you can do it too. Here are some places to start:

1. Tell your children today and every day how much you love them. Use both *words* of love and *deeds* of love.
2. Be civil with your ex-spouse for the benefit of your children and your own well-being. Reduce the anger factor.
3. Make a plan for spending time with your children each day and each weekend. You're less frustrated with your busy life when you make the time to be in touch.

4. Prepare a financial plan for spending and saving—and a budget if you don't have one already. Sure, it's not much fun, but don't put it off.

5. List the problems, putting them in order of priority. Then, start to tackle the first. Just writing them down will make you feel better since you have a foundation to build from.

6. Enlarge your circle of friends and take some time to be with them on a regular basis. See that your kids have social times, too.

7. Take a genuine interest in your children's school—be aware of home assignments, maintain contact with the teacher. Make plans for future education by setting aside a little "untouchable" money each month.

8. Get educated about and be alert to big problems such as drugs and alcohol, eating disorders, school truancy, premarital sex. Keep the lines of communication open.

9. Include your youngsters in home tasks so that when they leave home they know about cooking, car repair, sewing, home maintenance, laundry. Working together can be fun.

10. Keep your children safe—safety is a top concern of every parent. Be sure they know what to do when alone, when there's an emergency, when lost, and so forth.

11. Get your support group organized. Feel confident about your children's day care and your plans for handling illnesses or emergencies. Let others help you.

12. Don't plead guilty to being a parent with disadvantaged children, living in a broken family. What you are doing has dignity, and you are only guilty if you don't try to do your best.

13. Love yourself so much that you endeavor to replace any anger, loneliness, guilt, or frustration with forgiveness, trust, and love.

DO YOU KNOW HOW GREAT YOU ARE?

Many people don't have your ability to succeed. You do, because you are learning to be a great single parent. Read books, magazines, and newspaper articles, talk with other parents, spend time listening to your child.

Congratulate yourself on the smallest success. Remember that others have forged a path for you. Don't believe every gloomy statistic—in fact, work to change those statistics for the better.

Don't be discouraged by failures. Everyone has them. Successful people just don't let failures get them down for long.

When at home, regularly ask yourself: is what I'm doing the most important thing to be doing at this moment? Does it fulfill one of my goals? For example, do you persist in cleaning the house when a child is begging for someone to play catch? Put the really important things first.

Remember, childhood is so short. Make each precious day the best for your youngster.

Before you go to bed

You may be tired when you go to bed each night, but take time out to read this short prayer. Go ahead and tear the page out of the book! Put it on your night table. (Sorry, if this is a library book, don't tear the page out, make a copy!)

THE SINGLE PARENT'S PRAYER

Dear God,

As another day comes to a close,

Help me to be grateful for this precious child entrusted to my care.

Let me remember just one step forward that we've made today.

Teach me to reflect your wisdom in my daily tasks:

Teach me to praise what might go unnoticed,

Teach me to soothe the anger with hope,

Teach me to think of your power when frustrated,

Teach me to correct with grace what is wrong,

Teach me to love where there is hatred.

Bless those who are helping me along the way.

And also bless those who have hurt me, for they need your love, too.

And for the day ahead, bless me with

Strength where I am weak,

Patience where I am short-tempered,

Humility when I am wrong,

Faith to love and free my child,

Enthusiasm to live adventurously as a family.

For what is ahead is not a burden, but a privilege.

So thank you for letting me guide one of your children.

Please take my hand and guide me, too.

Let me awaken with joy, with hope, and most of all with love.

Amen and good night.

CHAPTER TWELVE

HELP!

Resources for single parents

THERE'S NOT JUST HOPE— there's HELP! Consider these avenues for increasing your parenting satisfaction and problem-solving abilities.

SUPPORT GROUPS

Parents Without Partners. To get the name of your nearest local group, call or write: 8807 Colesville Road, Silver Spring, MD 20910, (301) 588-9354.

Women on Their Own, P. O. Box 1026, Willingboro, NJ 08046.

Fathers Are Forever, P. O. Box 4804, Panorama City, CA 91412.

NOSM (National Organization of Single Mothers), Box 68, Midland, NC 28107-0068.

Toughlove International, P. O. Box 1069, Doylestown, PA 18901.

How to Grow a Parents' Group, CDG Enterprises, P. O. Box 97-B, Western Springs, IL 60558.

Displaced Homemakers Network, Inc., 1531 Pennsylvania Ave.
SE, Washington, DC 20003.

Mothers Without Custody, P. O. Box 27418, Houston, TX
77256.

Single Mothers by Choice, P. O. Box 1642, Gracie Square Station,
New York, NY 10028.

Military Groups:

Members of the military will be helped by contacting their base
operator. The operator will suggest where they should look in
their base directory. The following are the names of the support
groups for each branch of the service:

Army: Army Community Center
Navy: Family Service Center
Marines: Family Service Center
Air Force: Family Support Center
Coast Guard: Coast Guard Community Support Center
National Guard: Family Program Coordinators

Other Support Groups:

Your local telephone directory lists community services in the
front section. You will find local telephone numbers, helpful
information, and assistance by looking under these headings:
adoption, Department of Social Services, alcohol and drug
abuse, child abuse, family violence, women's resource center,
child guidance, family services, mental health, Regional Occupation Program, Planned Parenthood, health care, housing, Sal-
vation Army, legal services, youth crisis line, National Center
for Missing and Exploited Children, suicide prevention, U. S.
Veterans Administration, Big Brother/Big Sister/Scout/Camp
Fire groups.

PUBLICATIONS

The Single Parent. Published by Parents Without Partners, Inc., 8807 Colesville Road, Silver Spring, MD 20910.

Toughlove. Monthly, quarterly newsletters & manuals, P. O. Box 1069, Doylestown, PA 18901.

SingleMother. Just Me and You Kid Publishing, P. O. Box 68, Midland, NC 28107-0068.

Dads Only. Published by Paul Lewis, P. O. Box 340, Julian, CA 92036.

MW/OC Associate (Mothers Without Custody). P. O. Box 602, Greenbelt, MD 20770.

What Do You Do Now? Life Insurance Marketing & Research Association, Inc., Hartford, CT 06141.

Ours: The Magazine of Adoptive Families. Adoptive Families of America, 3333 Highway 100 North, Minneapolis, MN 55422.

SMC Newsletter (Single Mothers by Choice). P. O. Box 1642, Gracie Square Station, New York, NY 10028.

Positive Parenting After Separation and Divorce. PSC, 420 South Beverly Drive, Beverly Hills, CA 90212.

The Tightwad Gazette (how to stretch your money). RR #1, Box 3570, Leeds, ME 04263.

BOOKS

The Parents Without Partners, Stephen L. Atlas (Running Press, 1984).

Single Parents Are People, Too! Carol Vejvoda Murdock (Butterick Publishing, 1980)

Sharing Parenthood After Divorce, Ciji Ware (Viking, 1982)

The Kids' Book About Single-Parent Families, Paul Dolmetsch (Doubleday, 1985)

Formerly Married: Learning to Live with Yourself, Marilyn Jensen (Westminster Press, 1983)

Mom's House, Dad's House: Making Shared Custody Work, Isolina Ricci (Macmillan, 1980)

Successful Single Parenting, Anne Wayman (Simon & Schuster, 1987)

Raising Self-reliant Children in a Self-indulgent World, H. Stephen Glenn and Jane Nelson (Prima Publications & Communications, 1988)

Solo Parenting: Your Essential Guide: How to Find the Balance Between Parenthood and Personhood, Kathleen McCoy (New American Library, 1987)

The Daddy Track and the Single Father, Geoffrey L. Greif (Lexington Books, 1990)

Sex and the Single Parent, Mary Mattis (Henry Holt, 1986)

How to Become a Single Parent: A Guide for Single People Considering Adoption or Natural Parenthood Alone, Josephine J. Curto (Prentice-Hall, 1983)

How to Single Parent, Fitzhugh Dodson (Harper & Row, 1987)

Living the Possible Dream: The Single Parent's Guide to College Success, Julia Riley (Johnson Books)

INDEX